GUIDE TO FAR WEST FISHING

LOU WIENECKE
with
JOHN PETERSON

PRENTICE-HALL, Inc.
Englewood Cliffs, N. J.

G © THE H. M. GOUSHA COMPANY SAN JOSE
Reprinted by permission

Maps: California State No. 1036S
Oregon State No. 586J and
Washington State No. 587J.

Guide to Far West Fishing by Lou Wienecke
with John Peterson
Copyright © 1973 by Louis G. Wienecke
and John Peterson

Printed in the United States of America

Prentice-Hall International, Inc., London
Prentice-Hall of Australia, Pty. Ltd., North Sydney
Prentice-Hall of Canada, Ltd., Toronto
Prentice-Hall of India Private Ltd., New Delhi
Prentice-Hall of Japan, Inc., Tokyo

10 9 8 7 6 5 4 3 2 1

Library of Congress Cataloging in Publication Data

Wienecke, Lou.
    Guide to Far West Fishing.

    1. Fishing—California. 2. Fishing—Oregon.
3. Fishing—Nevada. 4. Fishing—Washington (State)
I. Peterson, John, date   joint author. II. Title.
SH464.W4W53   799.1'0979   73-9588
ISBN 0-13-369603-0

PREFACE

While writing this book we fished many of the streams and lakes, rode a party boat to seasickness off the mouth of the great Columbia, and slipped on a log while attempting to ford an ice-cold river in California. We'll take credit for any bum steers, but we must acknowledge the terrific help we received wherever we traveled. The outdoorsman is indeed an hospitable fellow.

Specifically, we extend our appreciation to members of the states' fish and game departments and to other knowledgeable fishermen. In Nevada: Tom Trelease, Bill Rollins, Kay Johnson, Pat Coffin, Dale Lockard, Bob Sumner, Joe Granata, and Avery Winnemucca. In California:.Ed Armstrong, Michael Johnson, Wendell Jones, Jim Ryan, J. Sheehan, Pete Chadwick, G. W. Ponder, Sy Nathanson, Jim St. Amant, Dan Christenson, Bud Young, Donald Weidlein, Elton Bailey, Phil Bartholomew, Elden Vestal, Ben Glading, W. Stanton Clark, Frank Hubbard, and Ben Marshall. In Oregon: Clyde Smith, Ken Cochrun, Frank Moore, Bill Salzman, Leonard Mathiesen, Vic Mason, Fred Locke, and Doug Yocum. In Washington: Jim Johnson, Roy Banner, Cliff Millenbach, Frank Haw, Reade Brown, Tom Knight, Jim DeShazo, Arthur Crews, Dory Lavier, Fred Holm, Carl Patzwaldt, Merrill Spence, Robert Hemstreet, Dick Simons, Bob Rennie, and Chet Gardner.

This guide will tell you where and when to go fishing. Its purpose is to act as a handy reference for planning your next fishing expedition or for finding fish when you only want to wet a hook for an hour or two as you drive the countryside on your vacation.

The search constantly gets tougher to locate good spots for fishing where a fisherman can find the wonderful mix of solitude, natural beauty, and sparkling water. Fishing waters become favorite waters for skiers and their power boats, pollution kills a stream, or perhaps too many fishermen have emptied a once-too-popular piece of water. And, just as important, you should know that Lake What-Do-You-Call-It has suddenly turned hot because its managers have freshly planted trout or bass.

We like to think of fishing, pursued with proper foresight and enthusiasm, as a true alternative to our urban life with its changing values, mobile existence, uncertainties, and unsettled character. The more we see of life and the more we experience new sensations, the more we hunger for new adventures and broader horizons. Because the level of experience between young and old seems to widen continually, this makes the universal experience and challenge of the outdoors even more valuable. Where else can a man and his son share the same meaningful times? Where else can a family spend days together, through common adventures and challenges? The beauty and pull each of us feels in nature is there for the others. Fishing is a great sport, but it also can be a great reason for getting outdoors, for creating real excitement, for finding family fun. Even a short mile-long hike off the busiest freeway gives the feeling that you might be discovering new ground, that you are seeing something few other folks could find.

The more you know of the countryside and of the fish you are after, the more you'll enjoy it. Study the habits of the rainbow or the salmon, learn the best lures and best spots to fish on a river. What counts most to a fisherman is to have his strategy prepared, to be on the best waters—and to net his fish. To hook a small rainbow about fifteen yards off the shoulder of the interstate is hardly the same as hooking the rascal on light gear in a pool just beyond a waterfall near the headwaters of the river. There is an unchanging majesty in any countryside; and the more you know of it, the more you'll feel at home and enjoy it. My uncle, a veteran fisherman and hunter, once told me, "I like to think all of my tramping around looking for quail and pheasant, sniffing out trout and catfish has taught me to think a bit like them. I like to think I can be a part of nature and that the beautiful country is a part of me."

We have relied on the local anglers and on the state fish and game departments for our information. And in all of these states we have talked to the department's local biologists, discussing with them which fish are planted when and where and which lakes and rivers traditionally yield the most and biggest fish. We extend our thanks to these knowledgeable people for their generous help. We've fished many of the waters ourselves and we want you, too, to get the thrill of the steelhead in Washington, the salmon in Oregon, the trout in California, and the bass in Nevada. All are great fighters and all are marvelously tasty.

We've tried to make this guide easy to read and follow. The maps are coordinated with the text, most of the larger towns, rivers, and lakes are set in large type. To see what we have to say about any piece of water, merely look for the larger type in the text. Right there we describe the best times of year to fish, the best bait to use, the points of access, whether rental boats are available, and detailed road directions to get you there. You should also check the legends on the maps. Each fish is represented by a letter (T for trout, for example) or letters telling what is on any stream or lake. The red dots are precisely located access points, often where there is a ramp to launch your boat.

We haven't worried too much about telling you how to fish. Most of us have our own secrets—if we can only find the fish. We have, however, included sections that tell you about the feeding habits of trout, bass, salmon, even steelhead. Be sure to read carefully what we say about the fishing holes. Some are merely mentioned, telling you what fish might be there. But other places, well, we've added a few descriptive words to let you know if this lake is the best in the state. We want you to be able to spend an extra thirty minutes or an hour to get to the best fishing in whatever region you are driving through.

So just obey the local angling regulations, take along a litter bag, spit on your hook, talk sweetly to the critters down below, and keep your face to the fresh breeze. Don't worry about the big one getting away—we'll find you another.

CONTENTS

CALIFORNIA   1
    Southern California   2
    North of Los Angeles   10
    The Central Section   14
    San Francisco Bay   19
    In the Salt Up North   32
    The Pristine North   33
    The Northwest Slice   44

OREGON   47
    The North Coast   50
    The South Coast   55
    Central Lakes   63
    The Remote Northeast   70

NEVADA   73
    The Huge Colorado Reservoirs   75
    Sparkling Lake Tahoe   78
    The Home of World-Record Trout   78
    The Trout of Eastern Nevada   81

WASHINGTON   84
    The Wondrous Olympic Peninsula   86
    The Puget Sound   92
    Southwestern Washington   101
    The Cascade Eastern Slope   109
    The Columbia Flats   115
    The Eastern Slice   119
    The Far Southeast   122

CALIFORNIA

This is truly the land of sun, sand, sea, surf — and fish. The Pacific, high-mountain lakes, rushing rivers, and matchless bays offer so much exciting water to the fisherman that he runs the risk of being intimidated. The key to success, as always, is to get on a piece of water just when the fish are hitting. You will find excellent fishing throughout this huge state at all times of the year, but often it takes some effort, particularly down south where literally tens of thousands of persons pack up the family car or camper and head into the countryside each weekend. We would like to guide you to places with both scenic beauty and fighting fish.

The best fishing is in the ocean, whether you are down south after the famed fighter, the yellowtail, or up north after the fifty-pound lingcod or equally huge salmon. Even the fisherman on a pier, jetty, or surf-spattered shore can expect exceptional success.

The freshwater fishing also sparkles. The prized trophies are the steelhead, salmon, largemouth and striped bass. The largemouth bass from Florida have been transplanted to many lakes in the back country above San Diego. The striped bass were transplanted from the East Coast to the San Francisco Bay nearly a hundred years ago. Both have thrived and have become great game fish here. Salmon and steelhead are natives and they just keep coming in greater numbers — and seemingly in greater size.

The best rivers — the Sacramento, Klamath, and Smith — yield salmon and steelhead from clear, tumbling waters coursing through beautiful, sheer canyons, and densely timbered forests. Other splended rivers — the McCloud, Fall, and Kern — offer fast trout fishing in equally glorious surroundings.

If the fishing were not so superb, the fisherman would still receive the tremendous reward of an outdoors experience in unmatched countryside. Or he could merely grab a pole and sit on the cement pier of historic Fort Point directly beneath the Golden Gate, drinking in the sights of sailboats on San Francisco Bay and the spires of the city's skyline. This is a state to be experienced fully.

SOUTHERN CALIFORNIA

A grizzled, white-haired gentleman in Los Angeles was telling us of his fishing experiences when he suddenly paused, scratched his leathery-skinned jaw, and asked, "Why would anyone want to waste his time on a puny trout when some of the fastest ocean fishing in the world is right here?"

Why indeed?

Charter boats heading into the offshore Pacific waters from nearly every "Southland" port seek out such storied fish as the yellowtail, marlin, wahoo, dolphin, and barracuda. Some boats will go out for only half a day, but others will range far down the Baja California coast on extended cruises after the biggest fish. The prized quarry here is the powerful yellowtail, a fighter ranked as one of the top five sport fish in the world. Only one out of five yellowtail hooked is ever landed. These fish will weigh up to forty-five or fifty pounds and they'll often yank line off a reel so fast it burns the fisherman's thumb and creates the disastrous, line-breaking bird's nest in a reel. The other great fish caught in huge numbers is the barracuda, usually off Mexico, except when they move north during warmer months. This is the only place the barracuda abounds in the numbers to be a prized sport fish. The marlin, dolphin, and wahoo aren't caught so frequently, but they're always a distinct possibility. Then, too, each year at the first of July, predictably, the albacore run starts north to course past Santa Catalina Island, lasting into September and sometimes as late as December. The big party boats — equipped for a daily happy hour and good sleeping — will fight the fifty, sixty, or more miles out to sea to find the fun. You've got to be a dedicated fisherman to put up with the rough water and demanding fishing. Most boats generally charge about thirty-five dollars a day. Closer inshore these boats work kelp beds for the white sea bass, which often weigh as much as fifty or sixty pounds, and other bottom fish. These white sea bass, particularly when they're small and caught inshore, are often called sea trout.

FISHING THE SURF

Though the shore-bound fisherman occasionally takes a good sea bass or barracuda, he'll ordinarily catch halibut, mackerel, bonito, barred perch, croaker, and queenfish. Starting to the south, spotted bass hit well in MISSION BAY and SAN DIEGO BAY, which again is sparkling after a concerted antipollution drive. The kelp beds off SAN DIEGO and LA JOLLA are traditionally good for bass and barracuda. The best surf fishing is from OCEANSIDE to SAN CLEMENTE, where there is also a fine fishing pier. The rock jetties at the new DANA POINT harbor produce halibut and perch. HUNTINGTON BEACH has a beautiful pier where anglers are modestly successful with perch and croakers. A kelp bed off LAGUNA BEACH helps the surf fishing there for perch, bass, and croaker. The piers at NEWPORT BEACH, SEAL BEACH, LONG BEACH, REDONDO BEACH, SANTA MONICA, and the private, fee pier at MALIBU can be good, but normally aren't because fishing has suffered from the metropolitan area's pollution. And don't forget that the famed, storied grunion run at night all along the sandy beaches during June and July. It's really true!

In Southern California the saltwater fishing is far superior to that in lakes and streams. The party boat fishing, too, ranks superior to that from the shore into the surf and off jetties and piers. The best skin diving on the West Coast is out at SANTA CATALINA ISLAND, though it's more for the photographer than the fisherman.

NOW FOR FRESHWATER FISHING

Freshwater fishing is mostly for planted trout, bass, and catfish. Heavy fishing pressure is par for the course, so be prepared for the throng. Two exceptions are the impounded waters of the Colorado River with fine crappie and striped bass, and the Salton Sea with huge corvina that have thrived there since they were transplanted from the Sea of Cortez about twenty years ago. The San Diego bass lakes such as Murray and Lower Otay produce bass over ten pounds for plastic worm fishermen every year, but local talent take the lion's share of these big ones as they reside in deep holes and along drop-offs that can be pinpointed only after many days of fishing effort. The traveling fisherman has a better chance of scoring in salt water or in the Colorado.

Starting in Los Angeles, just north of POMONA, you can head for Puddingstone Reservoir where bass and catfish can be taken. Heading north on Rte. 39, trout can be caught during the summer up the canyon where the SAN GABRIEL RIVER parallels the highway. Right there, too, is CRYSTAL LAKE, small but cool enough for trout. Perhaps a better yield of larger trout comes from Big Bear Lake. Try fishing off the old, low dam for trout to four pounds. You can hike back into the wilds here, following up the San Gabriel forks, or up Deep and Bear Creeks over to the east. This popular, scenic area lies to the northeast of San Bernardino and has good recreational facilities for the whole family. Throughout this heavily populated Southland you must reserve campsites ahead of time or at least stop by early or mid-afternoon. South of LOS ANGELES and east of ORANGE, IRVINE LAKE (or SANTIAGO RESERVOIR) produces good bass and catfish from mid-January through the spring. Rental boats and picnic tables are available on this private, fee lake. LAKE ELSINORE, thirty miles east of Rte. 5 on Rte. 74 yields bragging-size bass every spring. Boating and skiing pretty much rule the water during the hotter months, however. Continuing east on Rte. 74 you can find good summer camping and trout fishing in the San Jacinto Mountains at 4,000-foot-high LAKE HEMET. If you're east of the mountains on Rte. I-10 heading for PALM SPRINGS, turn for the San Jacinto Park, and you'll find Fulmore Lake halfway up the mountain in the middle of a forest. It, too, has nice trout. On a smogless day take the thrilling tramway ride above wild mountain slopes and canyons. Back to the southwest of the San Jacinto Mountains, you'll find private Vail Lake just east of Rte. 395 on Rte. 71. It's the kind of lake to be wary of — expensive, crowded, and over-sold.

THOSE HUGE SAN DIEGO BASS

Farther south, you enter San Diego County with its seventy miles of sand beaches. Bay fishing for sand and spotted bass is at times quite good in Mission Bay and the recently cleaned-up SAN DIEGO BAY. You should get current information from rental boat concessionaires. The Florida largemouth bass, transplanted to San Diego lakes, has inspired anglers to spend a lot of time probing the depths for a new state record. A seventeen-pound, four-ounce bucketmouth came from Murray Lake, north of Rte. 8. Also LOWER OTAY to the south, SAN VICENTE and EL CAPITAN to the east, and WOHLFORD and SANTA YSABEL east of Escondido are all possible lairs for a new state and, perhaps, world record. There are rental boats at all of these lakes.

North and east of San Diego, the SANTA MARGARITA, San Luis Rey, and Sweetwater Rivers receive plants of catchable trout from November to June. A call to the Fish and Game office to find out when plantings will be made would certainly be a good idea as these streams are pretty well fished out two days after a plant. The SANTA MARGARITA east of FALLBROOK would be the sole exception since you can hike in for a couple of miles to get away from the heaviest fishing pressure. State officials figure that ninety percent of all planted catchable trout are harvested within two weeks on most streams and lakes.

The COLORADO RIVER and its impoundments make up the California-Arizona border. (See the Southern Nevada map for

SOUTHERN CALIFORNIA

T	Trout
B	Bass
P	Perch or Catfish
C	Crappie
M	Offshore Saltwater Species
V	Various Saltwater Bottomfish
•	Exact Locations

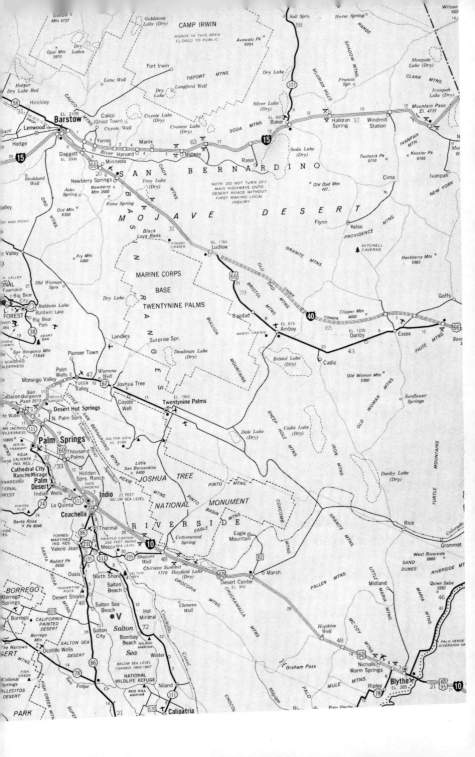

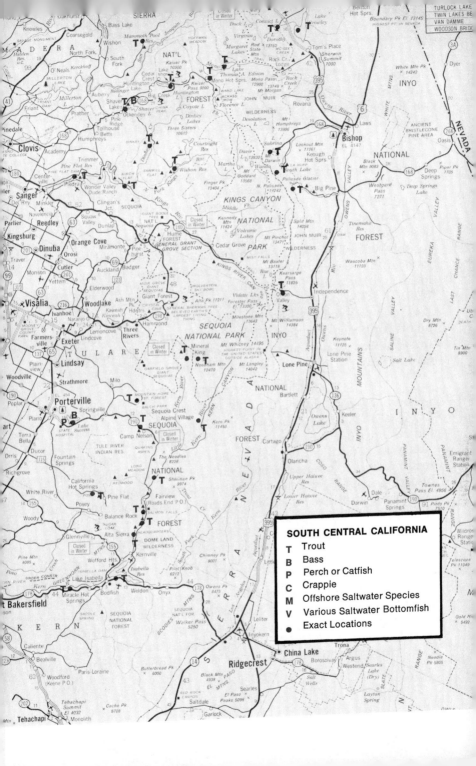

SOUTH CENTRAL CALIFORNIA

T	Trout
B	Bass
P	Perch or Catfish
C	Crappie
M	Offshore Saltwater Species
V	Various Saltwater Bottomfish
•	Exact Locations

Colorado River lakes.) The most famous stretch of water is LAKE HAVASU where crappie in unlimited quantities strike bait and jigs in the fall and in February. The best access points for boat rentals and launching are at Havasu Landing eighteen miles from Rte. 95 and at Havasu Springs over PARKER DAM on the Arizona side. Each spring, striped bass move north through Topock Gorge on a spawning spree. During that time anglers can do well trolling or drifting sardines for these ten- to forty-five-pound fish. Quite often the shallow-running stripers are visible from a boat, and they can cause wide-eyed fishermen to go berserk. Boats and canoes from NEEDLES and TOPOCK are favored for this type of fishing. Bonus catches of trout are also fairly common in the Needles area. Below Parker Dam you can stay at a lodge and bank fish for panfish. Or you can drive south to IMPERIAL RESERVOIR, another good lake in early spring and fall. Bass, crappie, and catfish of good size reside here. Your access points for boats, camping, and lodging are on the Arizona side at Imperial Dam and at Martinez Lake thirty-six miles from Yuma via Rte. 95.

THE CORVINA AND THE CATFISH

Heading west along Rte. I-8 in the Imperial Valley, the COACHELLA and all American canals hold big catfish throughout their irrigation waters. Check locally in the Imperial Valley at towns like BRAWLEY and CALEXICO for specific directions. Just to the north, the SALTON SEA still holds the rambunctious corvina, which can weigh up to forty pounds. Though the salinity of the water in this huge lake is rising dangerously, the fishing should hold up for a few more years. There are party boats and boat rentals available.

NORTH OF LOS ANGELES

Back in Los Angeles we will proceed north where the best fishing, of course, lies in the surf and out in the Pacific. But for freshwater angling, drop southwest of Rte. 101 at THOUSAND OAKS onto Rte. 23 to LAKE SHERWOOD, which produces nice crappie in the spring. If you want bigger fish, go thirty miles north on Rtes.

23 and then 126 to LAKE PIRU. Here you can find rental boats and lodging accommodations and, except for July, August, and September, pretty fair fishing for trout and bass. Just to the east of Rte. I-5 from Piru, you'll find CASTAIC LAKE, which has catchable trout. North of VENTURA, where Rtes. 33 and 150 join, take a short hop to CASITAS LAKE and enjoy fishing for trout in the winter, and bass and cats in the warmer months. A state record channel cat of forty-one pounds was caught here.

THE OCEAN AT MORRO BAY

The ocean fishing from LOMPOC north to MORRO BAY is more for warm-water species. Party boats out of Morro Bay occasionally take a two- or three-hour run to sea to fish for albacore, but most of the party boat action is for rockfish. The surf fishing is usually very good for barred surf perch and croakers. There are piers at Morro Bay and Pismo Beach. Every year about Labor Day the PISMO BEACH pier gets a run of barracuda that lasts for about three weeks. These waters, particularly farther south toward Mexico, are among the best in the world to go after barracuda. Just north of Santa Barbara on Rte. 154, all facilities, including boat rentals, are available at popular CACHUMA LAKE, which is well-known for winter trouting and large bass in the spring and early summer.

At Pismo Beach, where Rtes. 101 and 1 converge, the famous Pismo clams can be dug during the lower tides. The lower the tide, the better the clam digging. The Arroyo River and nearby OCEANO LAGOON are stocked with trout so you might consider a combination clam digging/trout fishing trip. And if you have a small boat, try your favorite weedless lure with the bass in Oso Flaco Lake a few miles south of OCEANO off Rte. 1. Traveling north on scenic Rte. 101, turn west about twenty miles north of PASO ROBLES, where you can launch or rent a boat and do well on panfish and bass in LAKE NACIMIENTO or SAN ANTONIO RESERVOIR. Excellent campgrounds with hot showers and swings for the kids are located at San Antonio. The more adventurous, who have car-top boats or rafts, will find springtime and fall bassing pretty good at HUNTER LIGGETT MILITARY

RESERVATION between KING CITY and Bradley. Hughes, Coleman, and Sycamore Lakes on the reservation are recommended.

THE SIERRA NEVADA TROUT

Let's go northeast from here and increase elevation. The wind-whipped San Joaquin Valley offers little in the way of aesthetics, but you can begin to breathe easier after you pass Fresno and roll into the Sierra foothills.

We're getting into good trout waters now. About twenty-five miles north of Fresno on Rte. 41, you should turn right on Rte. 200, go fifteen miles beyond O'Neal's to NORTH FORK. There, you have another thirty miles to drive over winding Rte. 100, directly north, to where the road bridges Chiquito Creek. You can take a right after crossing the bridge and find several campgrounds near the creek. The fly fishing for trout here is excellent, particularly in the fall.

From here we move into back country, where few people venture and even fewer pause to fish. This is the beginning of a high Sierra adventure. Returning to forest-lined Rte. 100, keep going up to the Granite Creek area about twelve miles from the Chiquito Creek bridge. There is a campsite there and a pack station nearby for acquiring horses and supplies. Late September and October are best for fishing this MINARETS WILDERNESS area. The lake waters are cooling off then, and the trout come into shallow water to actively feed. One good horseback trip is north of Strawberry Tungsten Mine Road into the Isberg Peak Lakes: McCLURE and WARD for brook trout, and ISBERG for the flashy golden trout. The stream below McClure should not be overlooked either. Driving back from Strawberry Tungsten Mine, keep an eye out for the road to Chiquito Lake. You can drive to within a couple of hundred yards of this trout-filled lake.

Going northeast on Rte. 168 out of Fresno, you can rent a boat to fish SHAVER LAKE with lures or bait for trout or bass. Shaver seems to have passed its peak, but occasional limits go to more experienced fishermen. You get into scenic high country driving farther northeast past the popular and fairly productive

HUNTINGTON LAKE and through KAISER PASS to Lake Tom Edison. You may prefer stream fishing to the trolling method used in Edison for trout. If so, stop just west of Edison in MONO HOT SPRINGS. Cabins, bathing, and campsites make it a comfortable location from which to hike into trout waters harboring wily browns up to seven pounds. Care must be used in approaching and presenting your bait to brown trout, for they are the smartest of all trout. Their phenomenal size is due to their shyness and reluctance to take bait which has a visible hook.

Drive southeast of Shaver Lake on Dinkey Creek Road to get to good fishing for trout in Dinkey Creek. You should hike a distance from the road. In the same direction, you have your choice of trout fishing in WISHON RESERVOIR or in KINGS RIVER above and below PINE FLAT RESERVOIR. Wishon is a favorite because it holds large browns to fifteen pounds and accommodates the traveling fisherman very well with nice campgrounds, trailer hookups, and boat rentals. KINGS RIVER is usually best in the spring and fall; but summer can be good too, if you can muster enough patience for the chancy strikes of twelve- to sixteen-inch rainbow. Horseback trips can also be made from MINERAL KING into the Sequoia National Park; and the headwaters of the Kern River can be rewarding, if not for the rainbow and golden trout fishing, at least for the scenic and invigorating countryside. To properly fish the area you should allow a week, but day hikes and overnight pack trips can also be arranged.

East of here on Rte. 395 on the other side of the mountains, you can make hiking and pack-animal trips from the ends of the roads out of BIG PINE and BISHOP. Farther south on Rte. 395, east of Sequoia, you can drive to trout-filled Independence Creek west of INDEPENDENCE.

Moving west again, you have a wealth of opportunities for trout in the LAKE SUCCESS area. A more relaxed, boat and bank fishing show happens through the spring near Porterville. The bass prefer single spins and deep-running lures. You can rent boats and camp here. Another spot is north of SPRINGVILLE where two small lakes support rainbow trout from summer until mid-November. Then, drive east on Rte. 190 to Camp Nelson, alongside the Thule River. This stretch is heavily planted with rainbows. You can rent cabins at Camp Nelson amidst towering redwoods.

As you proceed southeast toward QUAKING ASPEN, you will leave the oak, brush, and chaparral country and find yourself in the heavily timbered Sequoia Forest. Hereabouts is some of the best fishing territory you will ever find. You need horses to penetrate the wild Kern River Canyon properly as it's a long, rugged trail to the upper reaches. The Quaking Aspen Camp has stock available and guides who will help you plan your trip.

A few miles south of here the highway parallels the KERN RIVER for about twenty miles. This is popular water, and because of the great width and depth of the many pools some trout tend to elude the bombarding hooks and grow to over eighteen inches. Even bigger trout can be lured from the Kern upstream, a few miles off the road. A hiking trail leads north. LAKE ISABELLA and the KERN RIVER below the lake hold large populations of rainbows with a few browns to eight pounds. Usually, a big one will finally lose the contest in the fall when his attention is on moving upstream to spawn. The hook-jawed male is prized by trout purists who make a habit of releasing all large females.

West of here, the CALIFORNIA HOT SPRINGS area offers a relaxed setting with catchable trout eager to bite flies or bait.

THE CENTRAL SECTION

This middle third of California has the wildest variety of fishing waters. The high Sierra Nevada Mountains hold sparkling lakes and rollicking white-water streams; the flat lands of the San Joaquin Valley blend into the bayous of the San Francisco Bay's delta; great rivers like the Sacramento, Feather, and American wend down from the foothills; and then there's unmatched San Francisco Bay itself. We'll work into this section from the south heading up the coast, then shifting inland toward the mountains.

Driving north on Rte. 101, turn west at GREENFIELD onto Rte. G16, which leads into the headwaters of the ARROYO SECO in the Los Padres National Forest. A good jumping-off spot to hike into this really rough country is at Horse Bridge west of the Arroyo Seco campground. These coastal mountains have little in common with the lush, snow-capped Sierra Nevadas — they're forlorn and desolate but they also possess a strange grandeur and beauty, particularly in the canyons of the Arroyo Seco. What's more, all of these streams hold nice pan-size rainbows.

NORTH OF BIG SUR

Over to the Pacific, just north of the awesome BIG SUR coast, CARMEL RIVER STATE PARK at the river's mouth is a popular winter steelhead spot. After winter rains, a fair run of the steelhead come into the swollen river. Drive north from MONTEREY on Rte. 1 to WATSONVILLE and the PAJARO RIVER. This is one of the most underrated steelhead rivers in the state since it looks unfishable most of the time. However, bait and spin-glos, worked properly, produce good results. The lagoon upstream of Watsonville is excellent after a rain.

North to SANTA CRUZ on Rte. 1, the SAN LORENZO RIVER provides the biggest run of steelhead south of San Francisco. Access is best near the mouth at Santa Cruz. Fly fishermen score well on the east side of the lagoon, where the steelhead often weigh up to twenty pounds. Housing developments have injured the stream's fishery, and silt mucks up the water much of the time so you should check water conditions before getting your hopes up. North of Santa Cruz about eighteen miles on Rte. 1, stop at the Waddell Creek Bridge and check the fishing in the lagoon. Although the steelhead run here is dropping off, action has been good historically. The stream above the bridge is closed to the public.

SOUTH OF SAN FRANCISCO

South of San Francisco the ocean fishing centers around HALF MOON BAY and MONTEREY BAY. When the salmon are running, the party boats go after them. The rest of the year they concentrate on rockfish and bottom fish. The fishing piers are at Half Moon Bay, Santa Cruz, Monterey, and a private pier at Capitola. At the "cement ship" public fishing "pier" at Seacliff State Park

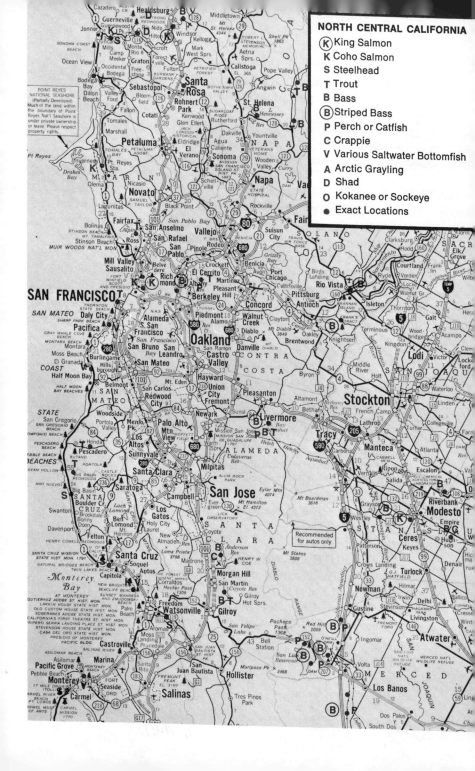

NORTH CENTRAL CALIFORNIA

- Ⓚ King Salmon
- K Coho Salmon
- S Steelhead
- T Trout
- B Bass
- Ⓑ Striped Bass
- P Perch or Catfish
- C Crappie
- V Various Saltwater Bottomfish
- A Arctic Grayling
- D Shad
- O Kokanee or Sockeye
- ● Exact Locations

just south of Santa Cruz, there's a good fall salmon run, but most of this pier — and jetty — fishing is for an assortment of perch and bottom fish. The best jetty fishing is at PRINCETON in Half Moon Bay. Monterey and Carmel have the best waters for skin diving north of Santa Catalina Island, but there are few abalone. Around Monterey barred surf perch are popular game, but the number one sport is for sand dabs. And of course, wherever you see a rocky shoreline, the rockfish abound. That kind of fishing is good at the base of Devil's Slide just south of San Francisco and PACIFICA, but every year about a half-dozen fishermen die on the rocks and surf there. One other unpredictable fish can be caught in the surf from HALF MOON BAY on up to BODEGA, but only in unusually warm years: This is the prized striped bass, and it's worth an inquiry to learn if they are hitting in the surf.

Striper and salmon haul from San Francisco Bay.
CALIFORNIA FISH AND GAME DEPARTMENT

South of San Francisco on Rte. 1, you will cross two streams planted in early summer with catchable rainbows, Gazos Creek and PESCADERO CREEK. The best spots along the Gazos are two to five miles up the road paralleling the stream. The most popular location on the Pescadero is about six miles east of the town of PESCADERO at the county park. Nothing else south of San Francisco is worth mentioning — except at the beautiful Crystal Springs and San Andreas Reservoirs, which support giant trout but aren't yet open to public use. In San Francisco you can find some pretty dependable trout fishing in Lake Merced, particularly in spring and early summer. There is bank fishing with bait, and boats can be rented. You'll have good company and competition from the old-timers who "live" here. A special permit must be purchased at the clubhouse.

Inland, south of SAN JOSE on Rte. 101, two lakes offer good spring bass fishing. COYOTE RESERVOIR northeast of GILROY comes up with occasional five-pound largemouths and also furnishes winter trout fishing from the shore. ANDERSON RESERVOIR east of MORGAN HILL has a boat rental facility off Cochrane Road. Some fast crappie fishing in the spring can be found around the flooded timber at the south end.

SAN FRANCISCO BAY

From just south of San Francisco Bay to north of the Canadian border, the anadromous fish are the most highly prized. These are the species that spawn in freshwater, head out to sea for a year or two to mature, then return uncannily to the same freshwater to spawn again. They spend most of their lives foraging in salt water, returning to the inland streams only to spawn — and amazingly in precisely the same stream or creek unless man or nature contrives to fool them. Although these fish are not voracious feeders after reentering freshwater streams, they will strike lures, bait, or flies more out of habit and instinct than hunger. There are four different anadromous fish in the coastal Pacific waters — steelhead, salmon, striped bass, and American shad.

The steelhead does not come into San Francisco Bay in significant numbers, but the colorful fighter is found in coastal streams as far south as San Simeon and the farther north you go, the more you'll notice the rambunctious fighter. Though the American shad can be caught in good numbers on the Sacramento River, after swimming through the bay, the two anadromous species caught in great numbers here are the salmon and the striped bass.

It has been found that *steelhead* in particular revert to natural feeding habits in the vicinity of their birthplace. Steelhead are a strain of rainbow trout, and the difference is primarily that they go to sea to mature and gain their extraordinary size, instead of remaining in a local stream for life as rainbows do. Strangely, steelheads are seldom found, much less caught, in the open sea. They are the most prized of anadromous fish, because of their bright colors, size, and fighting spirit. The summer run variety are smaller than the winter run, but they are more inclined to jump and are splashier fighters, though no more rambunctious. The winter runs are larger and more plentiful.

Salmon separate into an early spring-summer run and a late fall-winter run. Chinook or king salmon comprise most of the early run, with coho or silver salmon joining them in greater

Salmon jumping falls.
CALIFORNIA FISH AND GAME DEPARTMENT

numbers during the late run. Chinook are larger than the more aerially inclined cohos, but both are stout battlers. Salmon, like trout, go for pink-red food; and most salmon lures are quite a distinctive orange, much the same color as salmon eggs, which work well as bait. Of lesser value as game fish are the sockeye and humpback salmon.

American *shad* is another variety that comes into fresh water in early summer. They strike and then fight with ferocity for their size, which often is as much as six or seven pounds. A growing number of anglers fish for shad with lures and flies, particularly on the Yakima River in Washington and on the Umpqua River in southern Oregon.

The other anadromous fish of the West, the *striped bass*, is found in greatest numbers in San Francisco Bay. It was transplanted to the bay delta near the turn of the century, and its run there now rivals the salmon, though usually for a much shorter period. Stripers frequently weigh more than forty pounds and are particularly strong fighters. They move into bays and rivers in early summer, preferring to feed on herring, anchovies, and freshwater bullheads.

San Francisco's saltwater fishing in the summer and fall is usually superb for either salmon or striped bass. Charter boats are listed under "fishing bait" in the yellow pages, but usually people prefer Sausalito (Caruso's) for salmon boats and Berkeley (The Marina) for striper boats. It's a short trip from either Sausalito or San Francisco (Fishermen's Wharf) through the Golden Gate to the salmon grounds. And from Berkeley, striper boats go up toward the Sacramento River or into the bay around Alcatraz or Angel Island. "Twenty-pound" rods are used for either quarry, although heavier tackle is occasionally needed for the bigger king salmon and forty-pound bull stripers. In the bay, there are some good bank fishing spots. The mile-long Berkeley public pier is by far the most heavily used. San Francisco has a much smaller public pier, though fishermen also congregate at Fort Point beneath the Golden Gate and along the breakwaters of the marina. This shore fishing can be good, but more often it requires much patience to catch the perch, various bottom or rockfish and an occasional rod-bending striped bass.

THE EAST BAY LAKES

Del Valle Reservoir is the most productive lake in the bay area. From San Francisco drive east to LIVERMORE on Rte. 580 and watch for signs pointing to Del Valle Park. This lake — five and a half miles long — has everything — bass, stripers, trout, and cats. You can go there any time of the year and expect good fishing if the water is clear. Campgrounds and boat rentals are at the southeast end. Another good reservoir, San Pablo, can be reached by driving northeast on Rte. I-80 after crossing the San Francisco-Oakland Bay Bridge; take the San Pablo Dam Road exit. There's a nominal fee to use this cold-water reservoir, which is good year-round for trout and channel cats. Boats can be rented.

THE BAY DELTA

Fishing in the delta for spring stripers that weigh as much as thirty pounds is always popular. The striped bass were first planted here in 1879 when 132 small bass were brought from New Jersey and released near Martinez. After only ten years, striped bass had propagated enough to be netted and sold commercially in San Francisco markets. In 1935, however, commercial netting of bass was outlawed in favor of sport fishing. Fortunately for the sportsman, stripers prefer inshore, shallow waters, only rarely venturing into the deep sea. Summer and fall, as we said before, is peak time for bay fishing. Cut bait and bullheads are tempting offerings during the summer, and live anchovies are the favorite bait during fall months. During the winter, bass hold up in the bay and in the delta, but they don't actively feed during this time. The springtime spawning season lights their fire, and good catches show up in the delta and upriver to above Sacramento. Quickly retrieved plastic and metallic lures work better in the spring than the rest of the year because the bass have not yet established their feeding habits for bait fish. One of the best places is east of ANTIOCH on Rte. 4 to Cypress Rd. and on up Bethel Island Rd. to Frank's Tract. You can rent boats there. Another fine area is around ANDRUS ISLAND: Go four miles southeast from RIO VISTA on Rte. 12 to get to a rental boat and tackle supply area.

ACROSS THE GOLDEN GATE

To the north of San Francisco across the Golden Gate Bridge, three winter trout lakes nestle in Marin County's lush, majestic landscape. Beneath the towering redwoods west of ROSS, Phoenix and Lagunitas Lakes produce winter rainbows; while south of FAIRFAX, Bon Tempe Lake provides a relaxing retreat for those who will settle for catchable trout. Some people prefer this close-in fishing to interminable sight-seeing in the metropolis.

Further north on Rte. 1, turn west on Sir Francis Drake Boulevard at POINT REVES STATION. Less than two miles from town you can find one of the best silver salmon waters in the state, the mouth of the Lagunitas River. This is a tidewater fishery where the silvers get up to twenty pounds. Fresh salmon eggs, spin-glos, and spoons attract the silver salmon, especially two to five days after a fall or early winter rain.

Both Rtes. 1 and 101 cross a favorite San Francisco retreat, the RUSSIAN RIVER, as it meanders through coastal mountain canyons and stands of fir and alder. Drive to HEALDSBURG on Rte. 101 in the summer and rent canoes there for smallmouth bass fishing from Alexander Bridge to Healdsburg. There is fishing along the river and its feeder creeks, particularly in September, for big king salmon. A couple of miles north of SANTA ROSA, head west from Rte. 101 along River Road to reach the best winter fishing holes. Right by the Duncan Mills Bridge, a short road parallels the south bank of the river for one and a half miles. Exactly 1.2 miles from the bridge a cutoff road drops down to a gravel bar. Here you will find good water for silver salmon and steelhead. Flies, small lures, and bait can be used effectively. A good campsite a mile up from the bridge on the south side is a more popular fishing area. It can be crowded there, but limit catches are fairly common. In the same area, near GUERNEVILLE, a fine run of American shad inhabits the river from March to June.

On the east side of SANTA ROSA, there's catchable rainbow trout in Ralphine Lake, which is mostly winter sport. Between

Santa Rosa and NAPA, Rte. 128 leads southeast to an excellent big bass lake, LAKE HENNESSEY. Rental boats are there, and a fee is charged by the city of Napa for fishing permits. Keep going on Rte. 128 to LAKE BERRYESSA for outstanding trout fishing from November through March. Take the road from Turtle Rock two miles to where you see cars pulled off the road. There you can bank fish with minnows and a slip cork for trout four pounds and over. Along the same road you can find a campsite and boat rentals. Bass fishing in the spring is usually good in the Putah Creek arm at the north end of the lake. Also, here and farther south to Steele Park, trout fishing from boats is exciting in late October, November, and March when trout are chasing threadfin shad minnows near the surface. Troll a small silver spoon or fly cast into visible schools.

THE SAN JOAQUIN VALLEY

Jumping over to Rte. I-5 and then north on Rtes. 113 and 99, you'll reach MARYSVILLE and several top-notch fishing lakes. First, on Marysville Road, BULLARDS BAR has the trout-like Kokanee salmon grabbing trolled flashers in the spring, summer, and fall. Boat ramps and camps make it a good vacation spot. Farther down that road, Virginia Ranch or Collins Reservoir is best known for its trophy rainbows, though it's also fished successfully for bass. South of Marysville off Rte. 65 at SHERIDAN, take the Camp Far West road east to this lowland reservoir. If you're in search of nice striped bass and crappie, this out-of-the-way water has plenty of them in the spring.

Another lowland reservoir in the oak-studded Sierra foothills, FOLSOM LAKE, can be reached off Rte. 50 east of Sacramento. Folsom is perhaps the most popular lake for its size in the state with camping, swimming, water-skiing, and horseback riding predominating over the fishing. This is not to say the fishing is that terrible here, but you will have lots of competition for the bass, trout, and panfish.

South on Rte. I-5 out of SACRAMENTO, turn east on Rte. J10 at the Galt interchange, left on Rte. 88 for eleven miles to Buena Vista Road, and then right for three miles to PARDEE RESER-

VOIR. Water-skiing is outlawed, which makes it right for the serious fishermen throughout the summer. Smallmouth and largemouth bass abound, striking crawdads fished near shorelines and off points. Good numbers of Kokanee are harvested in the spring and early summer. Boat rentals can be found at the northern tip. A similar San Joaquin Valley lake with just as fine fishing, CAMANCHE RESERVOIR, is next door to Pardee just north of Rte. 12 near CAMPO SECO. On Rte. 12 south of Valley Springs, NEW HOGAN RESERVOIR sports hot crappie fishing and good bassing throughout the summer and fair trout angling earlier in the year. Driving southwest from VALLEY SPRINGS on Rte. 26, turn left on the road to Jenny Lind and at Milton drive east to Salt Spring Valley Reservoir. This reservoir is often overlooked in favor of the bigger waters to the north, but it can be very good for late spring crappie and bass fishing.

Driving west back to MILTON a road leads south to Eugene and OAKDALE. Take Rte. 108 from Oakdale to RIVERBANK. There you can launch a flat-bottom boat or raft on the STANISLAUS RIVER and make a nice, one-day float trip to the Rte. 99 bridge. This is good smallmouth water from spring through September. Below Rte. 99 you can float to Caswell State Park, camp overnight there, and go downstream to the mouth at the San Joaquin River for salmon in the fall months. This is a twisty stretch requiring a motor or a lot of paddling. East of Oakdale on Rte. 108 you can branch off the highway on Tulloch Road and do some bass fishing in TULLOCH RESERVOIR, which is a popular Stanislaus River impoundment. South of the Stanislaus another good floatable stream, the TUOLUMNE RIVER produces stripers in the spring and salmon in the fall. Boats can be launched on the west side of MODESTO and floated ten miles downstream to the Shiloh Road Bridge. Some anglers prefer the stretch of water below the Shiloh Bridge, starting at the confluence of the San Joaquin River. The best bass and crappie fishing on the Tuolumne can be reached by driving Rte. 132 east of Modesto about six miles to the Geer Road boat launch. This is a good access point financed by pari-mutuel horse-racing funds through the wildlife conservation board.

East on Rte. 132 to LA GRANGE, a few miles north and east puts you at superbly developed DON PEDRO RESERVOIR, which is equally good for the serious bass angler and the fisherman with a family to entertain. Or nine miles east of La Grange on Rte. 132 turn right to the Barrett Cove area of LAKE McCLURE. Boat rentals and hilltop campgrounds with hot showers and well designed campfire units make this a prime area for vacations or weekend trips. The fishing is very good for medium-size bass with an occasional five-pounder for the skillful angler. About six miles further east on Rte. 132, you can find another good campground at Lake McClure's Horseshoe Bend. Three miles further east you come to Coulterville. Take Rte. 49 south to Bagby and launch your boat for hot trout fishing in the spring.

FOR THE BICYCLE ENTHUSIAST

Turning back west on Rte. 140 through MERCED go four miles south from Gustine on Rte. 33 to Cottonwood Road. Turn right and go three miles to the California Aqueduct and a public fishing area. The fishing is good here in spring and sometimes in fall. Weighted anchovies are favored for catfish and stripers. The same type of fishing in spring and fall is popular throughout this area on the Delta Mendota Canal which is open to public fishing wherever you can reach it. Two more fishing spots on the California Aqueduct are located on the southern outskirts of LOS BANOS at the Canyon Road-Alvarado Trail junction and the Center Avenue-Mervel Avenue junction. Ten miles west of Los Banos on Rte. 152, the O'NEILL FOREBAY interrupts the regular Aqueduct channel. At the north bank of O'Neill off Rte. 33 there is a campground which is becoming very popular for bicycle riders who can peddle all the way from Grant Line Road west of Tracy. This is a 66-mile, black-top strip along the Aqueduct reserved exclusively for bicycles. Every ten miles along the strip are his and her toilets, fresh water, and wind-sheltered rest areas.

If you have a boat, you can launch it on the south bank of O'Neill or across Rte. 152 on pretty SAN LUIS RESERVOIR where bank fishing is also popular. The most productive area for bank fishing in the San Luis is off Rte. 152 on the north side.

Anglers take fantastic stringers of striped bass here in the spring. You must hike a short distance to reach the shore.

FISHLESS YOSEMITE

And now, hit Rte. 120 to Yosemite National Park. National parks such as Yosemite are hardly good places to fish because of a policy that allows many of the streams and lakes to be fished out and not restocked. This seems to be a shortsighted decision, but one that angling enthusiasts may have to work around. It is true that when Europeans first saw these areas a great many of the higher elevation lakes and streams did not support native fish populations; and it is the opinion of many that this "natural state" is preferable to the artificiality of planting catchable fish or even fingerlings in these waters. In a way, we can go along with that policy since the parks are being crowded by increasing throngs of visitors and added incentives such as good fishing aren't really desirable from management's point of view. But it seems certain waters could be managed as barbless fly waters for true sportsmen.

When you enter the park, you will encounter some of the most beautiful landscapes conceived by the Creator. The waterfalls in the spring and early summer lend power to this physical dream world. Many of the rugged cliffs and spires have never been touched by the hands of man. Drink in the sights and camp out under the sparkling stars, but unless you hear locally about good fishing in a certain area, don't bother to bring out your rod and reel. One spot in the park that may produce small trout is at TUOLUMNE MEADOWS on Rte. 120. Try hiking along the TUOLUMNE RIVER east of the meadows, picking your spots for trout.

Just a mile east of the park's boundary at TIOGA PASS, Lee Vining Creek has nice catchable trout. A mile upstream to the north, Saddlebag Reservoir also sports catchable trout. At the town of LEE VINING, you can go either north or south on Rte. 395 to reach hundreds of lakes and streams. We will only point out a few of the better ones, all stocked with rainbow.

First a loop road leads to GRANT LAKE, SILVER LAKE, and

JUNE LAKE — all with boat rentals. Further south on Rte. 395, turn to MAMMOTH LAKES and take your choice of some twenty lakes and streams around Lake Mary; or drive from Mammoth Lakes across Summit Road to the DEVIL'S POSTPILE and backpack into one of the many high lakes. Late September and October is the time to try for these rainbows. You will get a pioneer feeling as you walk amid autumn leaves in the glacier-carved meadows. A volcanic ridge overlooks the area and the blue lakes here receive very light fishing pressure. If you want the same sort of fall colors, but aren't up to backpacking, drive south another four or five miles down Rte. 395 to Convict Lake Road. A couple of miles from the main highway the very beautifulCONVICT LAKE offers campgrounds, boat rentals, and nice-sized brown and rainbow trout. Across Rte. 395 to the east, LAKE CROWLEY is popular for its occasionally hot trout fishing.

Back north on Rte. 395 beyond Lee Vining, go past saline Mono Lake to the Virginia Lakes Road, turn left for six miles to several campsites nestled amidst several nice trout streams and lakes.

THE FAMED GOLD COUNTRY

Leaving Yosemite and heading west, you will find a well stocked sixteen-mile stretch of the MERCED RIVER paralleling Rte. 140 from EL PORTAL to BRICEBURG. The bank's not too steep in most places to walk down to the river and pitch flies, spinners, or bait into the big pools. Some twenty-inch trout come out of the deeper pools. At Briceburg a good trail bike path leads off the road three miles west of town. This part of the Merced holds smallmouth bass. If you leave Yosemite on Rte. 120, you should check out the fishing at BERKELEY CAMP. You should be able to catch enough trout for dinner in this South Fork of the Tuolumne.

Driving west from Berkeley Camp on Rte. 120, Rte. 49 bends north to SONORA. From Sonora you can travel through the town of Tuolumne and go across a new road to CHERRY LAKE. It is relatively undeveloped, but it should become a favorite spot because of its large population of trout. You may have to spend some time trying to catch them because they are picky. Also, at Sonora, Rte. 108 leads to the east through CONFIDENCE and up to PINECREST LAKE, the STANISLAUS RIVER, and BEARDSLEY RESERVOIR — all with good trout fishing. At Belle Meadow four miles east of Strawberry, you can get outfitted for a horseback trip into EMIGRANT and BUCKLEBERRY LAKES where three-pound trout are not uncommon. Farther up Rte. 108 DONNELL'S RESERVOIR holds good trout. About twelve miles to the east at KENNEDY MEADOW, there is a resort and another pack station for horseback riding into the Emigrant Basin Area. Another twenty-six miles and you turn north on Rte. 395 to TOPAZ LAKE where you will find more trout.

Circling back by way of Rte. 89 to Rte. 4 you need only drive 26 miles west to reach LAKE ALPINE. There is a resort, good boat launch, and excellent fishing for rainbows and brook trout all summer. But back before the junction with Rte. 4, you can follow Rte. 89 north and for the first two miles venture into the Carson River for cutthroat trout. Turn to GROVERS HOT SPRINGS west of MARKLEEVILLE on Rte. E1 to find an area of quiet beauty with something for the whole family: A swimming pool, hot springs, campground, and the river well stocked with rainbows. Three miles west of WOODFORDS on Rte. 89 you can settle into another beautiful area with a camp at Horsethief Canyon and good trouting in the West Carson River. A couple miles west of the junction of Rtes. 89 and 88 you can take the Blue Lakes Road south to reach several lakes. The rough, twenty-mile loop, touches the UPPER BLUE and LOWER BLUE LAKES, both good for bank fishing or a car-top boat. At the apex of this loop, about twelve miles from the main highway, Sunset Lake road branches off south. You can hike from the end of that road a short distance to Sunset or Summit Lakes for brookies. Or you can walk a mile north to Hell Hole Lake or two and a quarter miles east to Raymond Lake to pursue the native, golden trout.

THE GRANDEUR OF KIT CARSON PASS

Returning to Rte. 88 where Red Lake banks the highway, prepare yourself for the grandeur of Kit Carson Pass with its monumental mountains rising steeply on both sides. On the west end of the Pass, TWIN LAKES or Caples Lake produces well during the season for trout fishermen. SILVER LAKE, a few more miles down Rte. 88, rivals it for fishing, camping, boating, and relaxing in a mountain resort. Enthusiasts even go to Silver in the winter to get to these trout. A high, granite, timbered mountain on the east side provides a beautiful backdrop.

ON TO LAKE TAHOE

Back at the junction of Rtes. 88 and 89, turn north toward LAKE TAHOE. This area is the most popular vacation spot in California. It certainly deserves the play it gets from sight-seers as Tahoe has the clearest, bluest water in the state, while Desolation Valley to the west has been preserved as a wild area; wheeled vehicles of any kind are prohibited. Eleven miles north of the junction turn left on Rte. 50 and stop at ECHO LAKE. From this point enjoyable horseback pack trips can be arranged for a week's

Catch of Brown Trout.
CALIFORNIA FISH AND GAME DEPARTMENT

outing among alpine lakes that furnish good trout fishing all summer. It's not very expensive because a guide can take you in, leave, and come back at a designated time. This is strictly living in the rough, because no cabins are allowed in wild areas.

Continuing on Rte. 89 you come to SOUTH LAKE TAHOE, and four miles farther you can camp at either of two state parks bordering Emerald Bay. Usually reservations are necessary for securing campsites. The fishing in Tahoe can be good at times; and deep trolling with flashers is the preferred method, shallow fishing being successful only during colder months. Most of the best fish are taken in the southern half of the lake where Mackinaw trout run to thirty pounds and Kokanee are a pound or more. There, at the south end, another Desolation Valley horseback pack station is available at CAMP RICHARDSON. A Forest Service center provides a slide show and short hikes into the area. Stay on Rte. 89 all the way up the west shore of the lake to where it doglegs away from the lake to parallel the Truckee River. Good campgrounds and fishing opportunities present themselves for fourteen miles to the town of Truckee.

To the north, DONNER LAKE yields a hundred thousand fish per year. It is only a couple of miles from the town of Truckee, and it has a Class A campground with hot showers at the east end. Boat rentals and a launch are located on the north shore along the old state highway. If you're up to matching wits with the smartest trout of all, the big daddy brown, go west from Donner Lake on the old state highway to SODA SPRINGS and turn south past Serene Lake to FRENCH MEADOWS RESERVOIR. A good boat ramp and campgrounds are located on the south shore. You can proceed another ten miles to Hell Hole Reservoir, which is not outlined on the map but is also good for big brown trout. A paved boat ramp is near the dam on the west end. The streams feeding Hell Hole at its east end are the RUBICON and Five Lakes Creek. In the spring, Five Lakes Creek holds good wild rainbows, but the only way to reach it is by boat. This east end of the lake is also good in late September and October for browns, particularly near the Rubicon Falls just south of the mouth of Five Lakes Creek.

Back to Soda Springs and on to Rte. I-80 past Truckee to

BOCA. You should pass up the reservoir here and continue for another eight miles to STAMPEDE DAM. Hard-surfaced boat ramps and a large campground are available near the reservoir's dam. Stampede turns out good stringers of trout for nearly anyone who puts a hook in the water.

A road angles around the north side of Stampede and goes west across Rte. 89 and about seventeen miles to JACKSON MEADOWS RESERVOIR. This country is laced with back roads which can be tricky when wet, but if you hit the weather right, take along a U.S. Geological Survey map and after sampling Jackson Meadows' trout fishing you can head south to Weaver, McMurray (which has a campground), Feeley, Carr, and little Bullpen Lakes, the latter holding arctic grayling. Car-top boats are ideal for these lakes.

If you have traveled this back road all the way you should end up at EMIGRANT GAP on Rte. 20. Near there, SPAULDING LAKE has catchable-sized trout and camping. Driving east on Rte. I-80, Big Bend also has camping and small rainbows in the Yuba River, which parallels the highway. Rte. 89 winds north out of Truckee to Rte. 49: Turn left here to fish the NORTH YUBA RIVER between SIERRA CITY and DOWNIEVILLE. About thirty miles farther west, Bullards Bar Reservoir sports a good boat ramp, campsites, and lake fishing for Kokanee. Some of the best lake fishing is north of here at Lake Davis and Antelope Valley Reservoir, which we cover in the next map section.

IN THE SALT UP NORTH

The ocean fishing along the North Coast often turns torrid, and, at its worst, is usually more rewarding than anywhere in freshwater. It is best from a party boat because savvy skippers know when and where to seek out the fish. The best action centers around BODEGA, CRESCENT CITY, FORT BRAGG, and Eureka where the boats go after big lingcod, salmon, and bottom fish. The silver salmon can run very heavily off EUREKA and FORT BRAGG as early as July, keeping up through the fall. It isn't uncommon for party boats to limit out within an hour at the peak of a king or silver salmon run. Kings average eighteen pounds, and the silver seven. When the salmon aren't running, these boats usually go after bottom fish and lingcod, which are highly prized here. In the spring and summer there's a good run of redtail surf perch from PT. REYES north, centering around EUREKA. They are around all year, and they'll average nearly two pounds with many weighing three pounds. Also in the spring and into the summer there's a run of rockfish near BODEGA. You can catch these fish near and over rocks, bouncing your bait up and down off the rocks. And you'll catch lingcod all along the coast, anywhere you find a rocky coastline, rocky reefs, and kelp beds. They average eight pounds, often going to twenty and forty pounds. There's also a lot of fishing from jetties and piers, though the catch here in proportion to effort extended isn't so good. You'll find piers at CRESCENT CITY, HUMBOLDT BAY, POINT ARENA, and the BODEGA BAY harbor. Jetties can be fished at CRESCENT CITY, EUREKA, FORT BRAGG, and BODEGA BAY. These fishermen can get into salmon in season, but usually their catch is of rock and other bottom fish.

THE PRISTINE NORTH

We will start this northern freshwater section on its south coast and move north to the Trinity region. Then we will cut back south through the central lowlands and finish heading north through the Cascade Range and the remote wilds along the eastern border. Here, in the far north end you'll find some of the most remote wilderness areas left in the country. There aren't many folks around, and the wild grandeur of the countryside matches the fishing.

THE ART OF STEELHEADING

Steelheading is a peculiar art of veteran anglers. There's much lore concerning the steelhead, and nearly all veterans have their own methods, which most pass along with relish. Generally, these fishermen fall into three camps, all of which take perseverance and patience.

First, the BAIT FISHERMAN relies on the steelhead's appetite for salmon roe. He drops a sinker of a half to six ounces, its weight

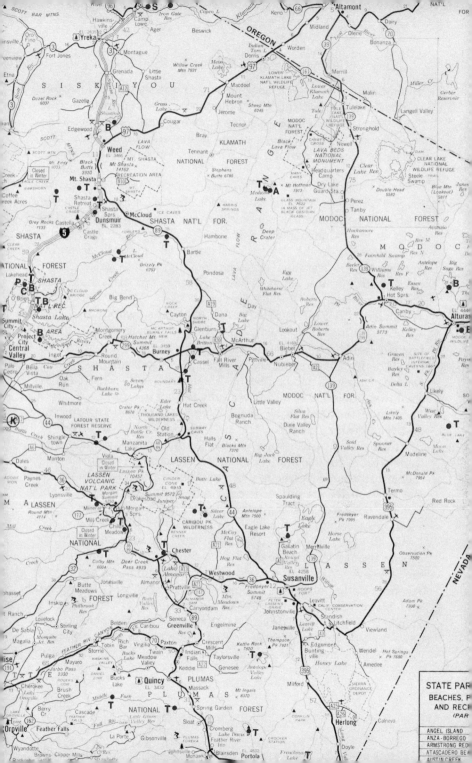

depending on the depth and current of the stream. The sinker bumps along the bottom, the hook moving with it only inches off the bottom. An old trick is trying orange or pink yarn around the line directly above the eye of the hook and salmon eggs. This tangles in a lightly striking fish's teeth and gives the angler more time to set the hook.

The LURE FISHERMAN, however, covers more water casting bronze spoons or whirling spinner-cork lures. Casting at an angle upstream, he recovers line just fast enough to keep the lure or the drop sinker bouncing along the bottom. He often works the brackish water in the mouths of streams, where steelhead prefer holding before traveling upstream rapidly, usually after a rain, pausing for minutes here and there by rocks and snags that break the current for them.

Finally, the FLY FISHERMAN is a purist who has usually spent a lot of time practicing with a shooting head (double tapered, weighted line) and studying the territory he intends to fish. The fly fisherman must be even more particular in picking water to work his dainty flies on. He normally fishes the quieter, shallower pools and small riffles found farther upstream.

Scenic Rte. 1 crosses all of the major streams, and car-top boat and bank fishing accesses are available on nearly all rivers. If there's a crowd of fishermen on one stretch of a river, make sure there's room for one more because steelhead run in schools. Some diehard steelheaders frequent stretches of water upstream where the fish usually are either present in large numbers or not at all, but the consistent fishing is in the brackish water near a river's mouth. Success in steelheading is measured by how well you can locate the fish. Often this requires hitting one hole on a river for ten or twenty minutes then moving on to another hole or even another river. Again, if you see a bunch of veteran anglers, don't figure to find a better hole of your own. They probably know of it and many more, and they aren't there for the conversation. A steelheader will often drive a hundred miles a day, checking out three or four different rivers. That's a fine technique in this area because in a stretch of seventy miles you can hit six steelhead rivers.

THE STEELHEAD RIVERS

The first of these rivers, the GUALALA, is tough to reach for bank fishermen because of private land holdings, including the sprawling SEA RANCH resort. For car-top boat fishermen, a good access is just west of the highway. Your next stop north is about three miles south of MANCHESTER, where you turn west to reach the GARCIA RIVER at several points. Some good, big fish hole up in the tidal section of this river. Farther up Rte. 1 at Rte. 128, turn east to reach campsites on the NAVARRO RIVER where the North Fork spills into the main Navarro. This junction provides good holding water for both steelhead and the small but frisky coho salmon. Next, BIG RIVER flows into MENDOCINO BAY just south of the quaint village. It's an art colony with galleries, restaurants, stately Victorian houses, and windmills. Your boat can be launched east of town off a road that branches off to the north at the Rte. 1 bridge. This is a spectacular stretch of the coast, a favorite of most Californians. Only eight miles from here, there's a boat access on the Noyo River right at the town of NOYO. The last of this cluster of steelhead streams is TEN MILE RIVER just north of Fort Bragg. In the winter, and especially in January, take a day's excursion on the Skunk Railroad that runs between FORT BRAGG and WILLITS on Rte. 101. Ask the conductor to drop you off at a good fishing hole somewhere between South Fork and Silverado Boy Scout Camp; the river is closed farther upstream. The train will be back through to pick you up in the afternoon. Fly fishermen favor this stretch of the Noyo, particularly when the river's down a bit.

South of Willits on Rte. 101 at UKIAH, MENDOCINO LAKE is best in the spring and summer for striped bass that weigh as much as twenty pounds. Rental boats and campsites are on the lake. To the south a nice side trip off of Rte. 20 cuts down East Side Road and the parallel Russian River. This water sparkles, perfect for fly fishing for catchable-sized trout. If you want bigger trout, rent a boat on nearby Blue Lake. Or, a few minutes south of BLUE LAKE lies picturesque CLEAR LAKE with unlimited numbers of crappie. They hit best from April through June. Lodging and camping reservations are sometimes necessary since this lake is very popular. Bass and catfish will often complement your crappie catch. The serious bass angler, though, should go a few miles south on Big Valley Road to launch a boat on Highland Creek Reservoir.

For a more pristine adventure, drive north twenty miles from CLEAR LAKE on Elk Mountain Road to LAKE PILLSBURY. Good springtime trouting is in the lake, and red hot summertime trouting is below the dam. Pillsbury's north shore is excellent for collecting pine, manzanita, and laurel driftwood.

THE MIGHTY EEL RIVER

Northward for forty miles over rugged, mountain terrain on an unimproved road you'll find the EEL RIVER to the east of COVELO. You can more easily reach this section of the Eel by taking Rte. 261 east off Rte. 101. Fresh flows from the Black Butte River spark steelhead fishing from March through May, though it can get too muddy even for bait and spinners. If so, head seven miles northeast to Howard Lake where eight- to twelve-inch trout are planted every spring.

The DOS RIOS area to the west is popular with Eel River fishermen in the late fall for king salmon and in the winter for steelhead. Steamrollers of twenty-five and thirty pounds are caught on roe and spin-glos. Go about thirty-five miles up Rte. 101 to LEGGETT for another access point on the Eel. Another favorite area is at Benbow where winter steelheading can be superb at the boundary hole below the dam. Keep an eye out for other Eel River access points between here and SOUTH FORK off Rte. 101. Cars pulled off the road indicate action spots.

Just north of South Fork, you might turn west into the back country along the MATTOLE RIVER near PETROLIA. Big steelhead can be found in December and January by going west along the south bank. Upstream, several holes can be found for bait fishing with fresh salmon eggs. Near the junction of Rtes. 1 and 101 and the mouth of the Eel River several holes have become quite famous for big steelhead and king salmon. These pools are called Singley, Snag, and Dungan and can be reached by driving north from Fernbridge. You'll have company there.

The best warm weather fishing in this part of the state is on the MAD RIVER. From ALTON on Rte. 101, take Rte. 36 to BRIDGEVILLE and then turn left to YAGER. From there, go east on the pass road, turning right on Stapp Road to Stapp Ranch. It takes a hike of more than a mile from Stapp Ranch down to the Mad River where you'll find wild trout fishing much as it was a hundred years ago. In the spring, Ruth Lake is a more convenient piece of good trout water. There is a campground between the lake and the town.

Ewing Gulch Reservoir — following Rte. 36 until the left at Peanut to Hayfork — is good bank fishing for trout at practically any time. Another twenty-three miles east on Rte. 3, and salmon fishing takes over. Both at DOUGLAS CITY and at Steel Bridge Road three miles upstream, you'll find access to the TRINITY RIVER, which has a fine run of spring Chinook in June. Both June and October are good months for salmon fishing at BURNT RANCH and at WILLOW CREEK farther downstream off Rte. 299. Sometimes the salmon run at Willow Creek starts as early as August, while the steelhead run hits here in late fall. Be sure to check the angling regulations for single hook restrictions and closures.

REDDING IS THE PLACE

Redding is one of the best jumping-off spots for fishing trips. Here, on Rte. I-5 three huge lakes and several rivers including the great Sacramento can be reached in a few minutes' driving. North on Rte. I-5 the town of MOUNT SHASTA acts as the gateway to the Trinity Divide lakes. Popular Castle Lake eleven miles to the south has good trout fishing in May, June, and October. The less heavily fished Gumboot Lake lies fifteen miles west of Mount Shasta in a rolling meadow. Give into the temptation to stop on the road paralleling a fork of the SACRAMENTO RIVER, which also offers nice trout. Halfway between Mount Shasta and DUNSMUIR the Cantara Loop road provides excellent places for wading the Sacramento in summer and fall. Below Dunsmuir the stream enters Castle Crags State Park, from which many campers explore the richly forested slopes and granite crags above, prospecting for garnet and aragonite.

Rte. 89 leads east to McCLOUD. And in a stretch of the McCLOUD RIVER from four to ten miles beyond town, trout slap flies, lures, and bait, particularly in the spring and fall. The best bet for summer fishing is ten miles south of town in the reservoir and in the Ad-Di-Na campground area below the reservoir.

THE FAVORED SHASTA LAKE

Northern California's favorite recreation spot, SHASTA LAKE, offers very good fishing almost any time of the year, especially if you hire a guide. One good spot to fill your needs, including guides, is on the upper Sacramento arm. Exit from Rte. I-5 just north of the bridge and go one and a half miles to the lake shore area, an area which yields especially nice crappie. Across the bridge you should turn at the O'Brien interchange to hit Bailey Cove. This popular spot — known for both trout and smallmouth bass — is replete with campgrounds, trailer hookups, a Pier 66 marina with rental motorboats and houseboats. The entertaining Shasta Caverns excursion departs from here each morning. South of the Pit River Bridge on Rte. I-5 turn off at Project City and go west to Digger Bay for camping, boat rentals, and summer fishing for trout. They'll even go for marshmallows here. Also, some bank fishing access can be found west of the dam. Eight miles east of PROJECT CITY, Jones Valley on the Pit arm has boat rentals and supplies. Here is where the serious bass anglers gather in spring and fall. This lake generally is best from boats as it has a sheer shoreline that fluctuates greatly due to water-management policies downstream.

Many other choice waters lie in striking range of REDDING. Nearby to the northwest Keswick Lake produces limits of trout in the early summer. And you can drive a little further on Rte. 299 and find plenty of trout hitting in WHISKEYTOWN LAKE in the spring and fall. If you don't have your own boat, rent one near the campgrounds on Brandy Creek Road or bank fish near the powerhouse on the west end of the lake. Keep west on Rte. 299 to reach the Trinity National Recreation Area. Two large reservoirs provide recreation for tens of thousands of water skiers and vaca-tioners. And there *are* fish. LEWISTON LAKE is a year-round hot spot for brown and rainbow trout. Campgrounds are situated on the west shore. This is good, fast-moving water for using spinners.

Then there's huge, 15,000-acre CLAIR ENGLE LAKE behind Trinity Dam and above Lewiston Lake. The west side of Clair Engle is better developed for camps and cabins. You can find full facilities at Trinity Center on Rte. 3 some twenty miles north of the dam. Largemouth and smallmouth bass hit lures and crickets best during spring and fall in Papoose Cove and Squirrel Gulch. Also, in late October and November, trout come up shallow and hit trolled spoons. A road leads west from the northern tip of Clair Engle and, though twisted and rough, it provides the main route to the Trinity Alps. Nearly thirty miles from Coffee Creek on Rte. 3 you will arrive at Big Flat. From here trails lead overland to lakes such as Caribou, Emerald, and Sapphire. This is rugged, back-packing terrain holding fifty-five trout-filled lakes.

Returning to REDDING, turn east on Rte. 44 and go past SHINGLETOWN to the Battle Creek Bridge. Pull your car off the road and wade up or down the creek for swift-striking rainbows. For fast lake fishing, turn north off Rte. 44 on either side of the bridge and in only three or four minutes you will arrive at Mc-Cumber Flat Reservoir. Pacific Gas & Electric has provided nicely laid out campsites and a boat launch. As with most fluctuating reservoirs, we advise hitting this one in spring or early summer be-fore the water level gets too low.

THE SENSATIONAL SACRAMENTO

From Redding, the options for the fisherman are terrific: Shasta, Clair Engle, Whiskeytown, McCumber. And we still have the best one left! Go about sixteen miles south on Rte. I-5 to the COTTONWOOD-BALLS FERRY exit and take the Balls Ferry Road to Balls Ferry. It's only five or six miles from the freeway, but this part of the SACRAMENTO RIVER is actually under-fished. Right smack in the middle of summer a man can rent a boat, proceed upstream or down, and fish some of the prettiest riffles imaginable. Husky rainbows of twelve to twenty-four inches take flies, bait, flatfish — just about anything. Chinook or king salmon can be caught here on a year-round basis — a unique phenomenon. Kings are best taken from November through February, however, when steelhead also run the riffles, snapping up salmon eggs. Like the Klamath River steelhead, these are relatively small steelies to eight pounds, though active fighters, full of spunk when tackled with six-pound line or a light fly rod. Everything is here for the fisherman — trailer hookups, motels, guides (which we recommend contracting your first time out), good eating spots . . .

Wending your way south on Rte. I-5, take the RED BLUFF exit. A short distance upstream from Red Bluff you will again find those classic SACRAMENTO RIVER riffles, which extend all the way up to Redding. Another eighteen miles south on Rte. I-5, take the CORNING exit to the Woodson Bridge. For half a mile above the bridge you can wade for shad in June. These are high-jumping, scrappy fish that readily take light-colored flies and small lures. From the same exit you can go southwest to BLACK BUTTE RESERVOIR; springtime brings crappies and striped bass into shallow water. Or take the road south through Newville and Elk Creek to Stoneyford and fish for Florida largemouth bass in EAST PARK RESERVOIR. A concession and ramps are on the west shore.

THE HIGH-COUNTRY TROUT

Leaving the lowlands, go northeast on Rte. 70 from ORO-VILLE into the mountains and the town of BUCKS LAKE. If you have four-wheel drive, turn right on Highland Road to the Little California Mine. Rainbows are thick in this boulder-strewn section of the FEATHER RIVER. Another way to reach the river is by driving through QUINCY and turning right on the LaPorte Road to where it bridges the Feather. From here you can negotiate the "shut-ins" (vertical walls of rock rising into the clouds) by floating in an inner tube. The Feather is a terrific river, but it's dangerous, wild, and hard to reach. East of here, near PORTOLA on Rte. 70, LAKE DAVIS is known as the "miracle lake." It's a flooded pasture, rich from the droppings of decades of cows, and it provides consistently good fishing for two- to five-pound trout. There are boat rentals. Another twenty miles east of Portola will bring you to the FRENCHMAN LAKE turnoff. There's good trout fishing here too, but the fish are smaller.

Instead of following Rte. 70 when it bends east, you can head north to CRESCENT MILLS and turn toward ANTELOPE VALLEY RESERVOIR for truly superb trouting and excellent camping. This is fantastic fishing, and the locals make it a must in spring and fall. Above Antelope Valley, famed Lassen County greets the traveler with plenty of wide-open spaces for family road trips and hikes. LASSEN NATIONAL PARK, a hiker's paradise, is here with its granite and volcanic rock formations. If you don't care how many fish you catch, arm yourself with a fishing rod and plenty of hot dogs and venture into the park's high country.

Most people, however, want to use their fishing poles for more than walking sticks and, east of the park, EAGLE LAKE gives them action in spring and fall. Lodging, boat rentals, campgrounds, and large Lahontan cutthroat trout to eight pounds make the stay complete. Summertime means warmer water, which usually turns off the trout, but in the same area off Rte. 44, SILVER LAKE holds up well throughout the season. And from the nice campgrounds here you can take day hikes into the Caribou Wilderness lakes such as Long, Turnaround, Black, Gem, and Cowboy.

Stream fishermen would do best to wade either the FEATHER RIVER at CHESTER or DEER CREEK along Rte. 32, south of the park. BATTLE, MILL, and GURNSEY CREEKS near the town of MINERAL also provide fast action on spinners and worms.

The choicest water in this area for fly fishing lies north of Lassen Park. Here, where Rte. 299 bridges HAT CREEK, you can wade up- or downstream for large trout. Check the angling regulations for special limits. Baum Lake to the south holds gargantuan browns to twenty-three pounds! But, unfortunately, interference from a growing population of bullheads is decreasing the lake's trout production. Below Baum, on Hat Creek you can walk between the bridges and take limits of medium-sized trout on spinners. North of here at GLENBURN some of the prettiest water on the earth is found in the FALL RIVER. A lodge there caters to fly enthusiasts from all over the world.

Driving northeast on Rte. 299 to ALTURAS you can take day trips to several bass and trout lakes which receive relatively light pressure. The most remote point from here is reached by driving south on Rte. 395 to LIKELY, turning east five miles and south another twelve miles to BLUE LAKE. You can fish from the bank, or put in your boat from a rough launch. Trout get up to ten pounds. Closer to Alturas, DORIS and BIG SAGE RESERVOIRS sport bass to six pounds. For trout, head west of Canby for six miles to Duncan Reservoir, which turns hot for both bank fishermen and the angler with a car-top boat.

Farther along on Rte. 139, toward the Oregon border just south twenty-five miles from the town of TULELAKE, take Hill Road to MEDICINE LAKE. This is summer trout action. This road, which winds through high lava beds, snowy at times may not be open before late June. Bonuses for fishermen are nearby Little Medicine and Bullseye Lakes, which hold prized arctic grayling.

THE NORTHWEST SLICE

Starting out with the coastal waters just north of EUREKA near ARCATA, you can fish MAD RIVER for the peak of the salmon run in November or for steelhead in the winter. Several steelhead holes can be reached by bank fishermen at BLUE LAKE and downstream to the Rte. 101 bridge. North Bank Road and Warren Creek Road also lead to angling access points. And just north of the Rte. 101 bridge a road leads to the mouth where you can launch a boat.

North about thirty-five miles, Rte. 101 skirts the shores of BIG LAGOON. You can search the shores for redwood and madrona driftwood and fish for starry flounder and small steelhead. Nearby FRESHWATER LAGOON rates the nod in summer for twelve- to eighteen-inch trout. You can launch a boat or fish from the bank.

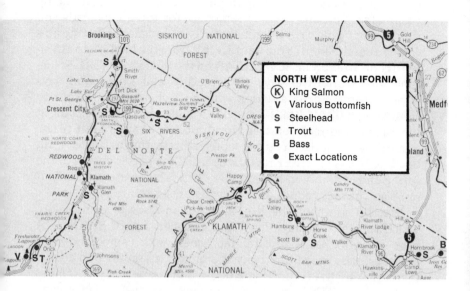

THE KING KLAMATH

Traveling north twenty miles beyond ORICK, the state's second largest river, the KLAMATH, flows to the Pacific. Renowned for runs of forty-pound king salmon and three- to ten-pound steelhead, you might catch one from August through March. Numerous access points can be found along the river's meandering course, but generally the salmon action and early fall steelhead runs are best near the mouth where guided boats are available. If the steelhead or salmon aren't cooperating, try the roadside area a couple of miles north of Requa on Rte. 101 for catchable trout.

Later in October, you should move upstream to around WEITCHPEC for steelhead. Or you could try trout-filled Fish Lake, which should live up to its name for you. (At Weitchpec, you can pick up Rte. 96 north, which parallels it to Iron Gate Reservoir at the Oregon border 140 miles away.) Also, in the fall, the stretch of the Klamath River by HAPPY CAMP pays big dividends for steelheaders willing to hire a guide. While in the Happy Camp area, you might enjoy searching for top-quality jade and rhodonite if you have the time. Plenty of lodging and campsites can be found here. If you want to fish from the bank go to HAMBURG on Rte. 96 or SCOTT BAR on the SCOTT RIVER. Sometimes the Scott River pays off especially well a couple of days after a storm. For late season winter steelheading, go north to HORNBROOK off Rte. I-5 and hire a guide, or try bank fishing at the Klamathon racks east of Hornbrook or at a pool just to the east of the I-5 bridge. You can score in this section as late as April, but IRON GATE RESERVOIR is usually a better choice in the spring and certainly in the summer. This is bass water with a boat ramp and picnic grounds on the northwest shore.

Rte. I-5 south of the Rte. 96 junction leads to many lakes, which turn hot in May, June, and October. LAKE SHASTINA near Rte. I-5 has a private, fee access with camps and boat launches. Bass prowl the rocky shorelines. If you're up to hiking, take the YREKA turnoff on Rte. I-5 and travel thirty-two miles on Rte. 3 to ETNA. Here you can make arrangements for pack trips into the Marble, Scott, and Salmon mountains high lake country. The Somes Bar-Etna Road wends its way high into the mountains and provides access to many campgrounds, pack stations, and trials to such lakes as Hogan, Chimney Rock, Steinacher, Clear, and Lost lakes. You will find this retreat a scenic wonder of wild flowers, spruce trees, and glacier-carved bluewater lakes and streams.

Back to the coast at CRESCENT CITY, the summer action is primarily party boat salmon fishing. Later, the salmon migrate to the SMITH RIVER. Before the first big rain in late October or November, you should hire a guide if you want the best chance at these fifty- to sixty-pound slabsides. A really heavy rain buoys all the fish out of this area so your timing is important. Drive south twelve miles on Rte. 197 to Jedediah Smith State Park and bank fish for steelhead in December; or take the Mill Creek Road further south for other access points. Also, you can find campgrounds and fishing holes along Rte. 199 as far up as Patrick Creek.

OREGON

The Rogue is one of the storied rivers of the West. Its fame grew early in the century when Zane Grey, a great outdoorsman who originated the Western novel, immortalized its beauty, wild waters, and fighting fish. Today, the Rogue is a favorite for boatmen seeking white-water rapids and calm, relaxing stretches meandering through towering pines and firs. It is, too, just as much a favorite for fishermen as it was in Zane Grey's day. Many of the fishing holes Grey liked still carry the names he gave them.

The waters of the Rogue never turn prettier than in early fall. At the entrance to the Rogue River National Forest, a willowy brunette told us enthusiastically about several beautiful campsites near its headwaters. We were about eighty miles northeast of Medford in the rugged, dense forests that form these tinkling waters. She had directed us up Rte. 230 and beyond two campgrounds with a few folks in them. The maps will show the Rogue to the west of the road, but we followed a sign pointing to the east and after two miles were in Hammaker Campground. There we enjoyed a pristine isolation with the Rogue only a few feet distant. It's about ten yards wide here, fast moving and sparkling clear, too deep to pull chest-high waders out of the car. The country is

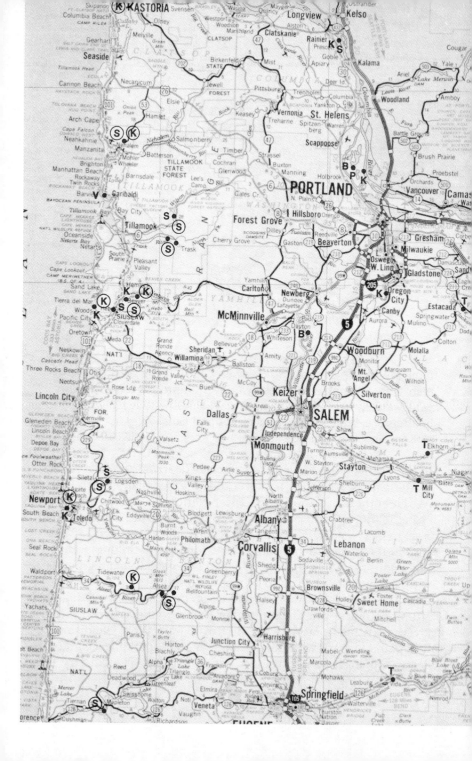

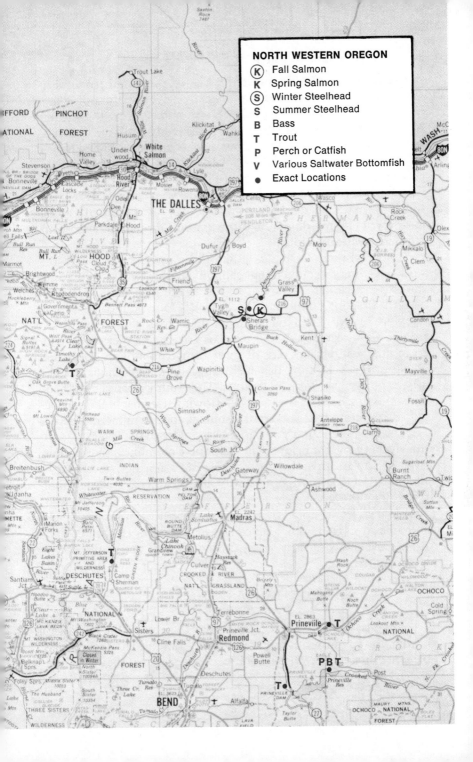

NORTH WESTERN OREGON

- (K) Fall Salmon
- K Spring Salmon
- (S) Winter Steelhead
- S Summer Steelhead
- B Bass
- T Trout
- P Perch or Catfish
- V Various Saltwater Bottomfish
- ● Exact Locations

rugged, hilly, and lushly forested — a setting so superb, so refreshing that my adrenalin was pumping strongly. It only took a moment to bait my hook with salmon eggs and cast into the stream. The trout hit my second cast, and I was ready for him. The wildness of the river infected the trout, for he was game. For an hour I enjoyed the heady pleasures of wild fish on a wild river in wild country. I had five nice rainbows, all about twelve inches. I didn't even heed the urge to move a hundred yards upstream where I had spotted what appeared to be a great pool at the bottom of a green meadow. I had my dinner, and those trout, dipped in butter and cornmeal, were delicious.

The fishermen of Oregon — like those throughout the northwest — get very excited about salmon and steelhead fishing. But the experience here is varied. In the fertile high desert lakes of eastern Oregon, rainbow trout grow to four pounds in only a couple of years. The bass fishing in these lakes also turns torrid, though the most noted is in Siltcoos Lake just a quarter-mile in from the Pacific where bass of three to five pounds are common. The northeast section has high, rugged, mountainous terrain where purists can lose themselves. The trout are wily, and there are some steelhead in the fast, free-flowing streams. In the central part of the state bass and trout fishing is good in numerous lakes. But for the best action you should stay close to the Pacific — and the rivers that flow into it. The majestic Columbia is the mother river of the northwest, setting the state's northern boundary. Steelhead and salmon run heavily in its waters, feeding other rivers like the John Day upstream. The Alsea, Nestucca, and Nehalem rivers are noted for sea-run cutthroat, salmon, steelhead, and rainbow trout. The glamor streams like the Deschutes and Rogue rivers have just as good fishing, despite the many whitewater sportsmen.

THE NORTH COAST

From just south of San Francisco Bay to north of the Canadian border, the anadromous fish are the most wanted. This is certainly true in Oregon: In these Pacific coast streams they are the steelhead, salmon, sea-run cutthroat, and striped bass — an import a century ago from the East Coast that has thrived. They spend most of their lives foraging in saltwater, returning to freshwater streams to spawn — many times in precisely the same stream and creek where they began life. Although these fish are not voracious feeders after re-entering freshwater streams, they will strike lures, flies, and bait, more often out of habit and instinct than hunger. It has been found that steelhead in particular revert to natural feeding habits in the vicinity of their birthplace. Steelhead are a strain of rainbow trout, and the difference is primarily that they go to sea to mature and gain their extraordinary size, rather than remaining in a local stream for life as rainbows do. Strangely, steelhead are seldom found, much less caught, in the open sea. They are the most prized of anadromous fish, because of their bright colors, size, and fighting spirit. The summer run variety are smaller than the winter run, but they are more inclined to jump and are splashier fighters, though no more rambunctious. The winter runs are larger and more plentiful.

Salmon separate into an early spring-summer run and a late fall-winter run. Chinook or king salmon comprise most of the early run, with coho or silver salmon joining them in greater numbers for the late run. Chinook are larger than the more aerially inclined cohos, but both are stout battlers. Salmon, like trout, go for pink-red food; and most salmon lures are a distinctive orange, much the same color as salmon eggs, which work well as bait. Of lesser value as game fish are the sockeye and hump-back salmon.

Shad is another variety that comes into freshwater in early summer. They strike and then fight with ferocity for their size, which often is as much as six or seven pounds. A growing number of anglers fish for shad with lures and flies, particularly on the Yakima River in Washington and on the Coos and Umpqua Rivers in southern Oregon.

The other anadromous fish of the west, the *striped bass*, is found in greatest numbers in San Francisco Bay. It was transplanted to the bay delta near the turn of the century, and its run there now rivals the salmon, though usually for a much shorter period. Stripers frequently weigh more than forty pounds and are particularly strong fighters. They move into bays and rivers in early summer, preferring to feed on herring, anchovies, and fresh-water bullheads.

The Columbia River is the greatest thoroughfare in the United States for anadromous fish. Giant salmon run up against its current from spring to fall; and steelhead up to thirty pounds cruise in from the Pacific and make much the same run as the salmon to spawning gravel in tributary streams. Sandbars along the banks of the Columbia provide ideal fishing spots for plunking with lures or fresh salmon eggs. Off the mouth of the river and along the Pacific coast, salmon fishermen flock to party boats out of Astoria and most towns farther south throughout the spring, summer, and fall. Newport, like other ocean ports, is a competitive place for charter boat fishermen: One charter skipper, attempting to lure more than his share of anglers, announced that he would use "topless bait girls."

Nearly all coastal streams support salmon, steelhead, and the native cutthroat trout, which can be found normally from August through October in the tidewaters. It's mostly a boat show, trolling spinners, for these small but scrappy sea-run fish known for their aerial acrobatics. The Alsea, Nestucca, and Nehalem rivers are cold-weather favorites for steelhead and salmon. The name McKenzie conjures all kinds of fond memories for anyone who has used the famed McKenzie River boat for drift fishing or white-water sport boating. The native rainbows in the McKenzie are so brightly colored that the locals dub them "redsides," and in order to protect the brood stock, a "throw back if over fourteen inches" rule exists. The McKenzie, therefore, is the river for the sportsman who wishes to test his skill against wily, hooked-before rainbows that know most of the tricks. For bass the noted Siltcoos Lake is on the central coast, a beautiful natural lake only two miles from the open sea. The bass get up to ten pounds here.

SALMON IS THE SPORT

In Oregon, salmon are more the fish than steelhead. From towns all along this North Coast party boats put out to sea daily from spring to late fall to search out salmon. And they have great success. Astoria traditionally brings in the largest catch, but boats also do extremely well from such places as WARRENTON, NEWPORT, and DEPOE BAY. This is ocean trolling and mooching with spoons and bait. The party boats can provide all the gear you'll need, but you should prepare yourself for the open rough waters and chilly temperatures, particularly watching your diet the night before if swells and chops give you trouble.

You could, alternately, try bank or sandbar fishing, which is good during the spring and summer at PRESCOTT and Sauvie Island just north of PORTLAND on the Columbia. Equip yourself with medium-weight spinning or casting gear, and take along a couple of terminal rigs for plunking on the bottom. All sporting goods stores here carry them. Plunking takes patience but it rewards the fisherman well. If you are near the Sauvie Island sandbar, it's only a couple of minutes to Sturgeon Lake, where the catfish, bass, and perch give fast action, particularly for those in boats. And right here, too, the WILLAMETTE RIVER joins with the Columbia, moving up from the south through Portland. The best area is usually just below the OREGON CITY dam where big Chinook strike often during the spring months. This spot, though, is very much a "suicide row" or "hog line" of boats when the Chinook are hitting, and you'd best have some experience to barge into that kind of competitive action. Ten years ago, the Willamette was heavily polluted. The fishing had been decimated by industrial, municipal, and agricultural wastes pumped carelessly into the river. Today ninety percent of the pollution has been diverted and not only can you fish for Chinook, you can swim in the river. The cleansing action was a result of a concerted drive by fishermen, industrialists, government officials, and conservationists. The big problem here is one of access to the river, but that problem is common on most rivers in Oregon.

West of Portland on the coast, the NORTH FORK of the NEHALEM RIVER supports nice runs of coho salmon and winter steelhead. You can fish from the bank at numerous spots northeast of NEHALEM, all of which are accessible from Rte. 53. Some people like to fish in the rocks and off the jetties for lingcod and other bottom fish in the ocean. One of the best spots for this usually excellent fishing is off the jetty at Barview County Park just ten miles south of Nehalem. The jetty juts into TILLAMOOK BAY, which is fed by two superb streams, the WILSON RIVER and the TRASK RIVER. The Wilson is a top-notch winter and summer steelhead stream, the local fishermen usually working it about fifteen miles upstream to the east. Your best chance is to fish wherever the other fishermen — and their cars — have gathered along Rte. 6. Steelhead seem to congregate and when one stretch of a river is hot, another probably is not. A road parallels much of the Trask River to the town of TRASK, but we'd recommend heading east until you hit the bank-fishing spots at the old county park and at the old Girl Scout camp, which are both within three miles of the town of Trask.

SALMON IN THE SURF

For a thrilling change of pace, drive on south to Cape Kiwanda by PACIFIC CITY. There the steep-sided dory boats bob, weave, and lurch in the surf, the fishermen commercially working for salmon. A dory boat rental is available to anyone who wants that kind of rough, demanding action. Just five miles south, probably the best all-around coastal stream flows into the sea: The NESTUCCA RIVER offers exciting fishing for salmon, steelhead, and cutthroat. You can bank fish or take out a drift boat west of HEBO (along Rte. 101) at the mouth of Three Rivers. Or you can put a boat in at the first, second, or fourth bridges east of BEAVER. Also, a good bank fishing spot is at the mouth of Beaver Creek at Beaver, though you should again look for the cars along the road.

The salmon fishing also sparkles at NEWPORT and DEPOE BAY. The shortest river in the world may be here. Slightly north of Depoe Bay, a tiny stream officially named "D River" gurgles the 440 feet — that's at low tide; the river is even shorter at high tide — from Devil's Lake to the Pacific Ocean in Lincoln City. Chinook and jack salmon have made the short trip from the ocean to the lake for years. Steelheading in the SILETZ RIVER, to the southeast, peaks in September and December with most of the action coming on lures and fresh salmon eggs. You can reach the bank between SILETZ and LOGSDEN at numerous places. Just a few miles south of Newport, bank fishermen do well on the ALSEA RIVER both above and below the town of ALSEA. A relatively unknown stretch of water, Fall Creek, empties into the Alsea River downstream from the town. Take the Fall Creek Road north from Rte. 34, picking the riffle that looks best. The last river in this section, the Siuslaw, is probably as good for cutthroat as any, and it also has a nice run of winter steelhead. The cutthroat hit best near its mouth at FLORENCE, while the best steelheading is normally upstream near SWISSHOME. A good boat trip would start at Swisshome on Rte. 126 and run to MAPLETON. Here, too, is SILTCOOS LAKE where there is a fine resort and superb bass fishing in the spring. The perch and bullhead bite through the summer.

WILLAMETTE TRIBUTARIES

Moving inland to the east of Rte. I-5 and SPRINGFIELD, the famed MCKENZIE RIVER sports its kaleidoscopic "redside" rainbow trout. The town of Vida is at the center of one of the more popular stretches, but we'd recommend a guide for the rugged McKenzie. They come reasonably, and it's a memorable river trip.

Just off the WILLAMETTE RIVER near ST. PAUL, is Lambert Slough, which is good boating for bass. Just south, out of Salem, the best bets for trout fishing will be along Rte. 22 in the SANTIAM RIVER and along Alkhorn Road in the LITTLE NORTH SANTIAM. Both produce well from opening day to mid-June. Again, you must check seasons and limits because they are changeable.

THE SOUTH COAST

Any time is the right time to catch them jumping hereabouts: In the fall, sea-run cutthroat and salmon; in the winter, steelhead; in the spring, salmon and striped bass to sixty pounds;

SOUTH WEST OREGON

K	Spring Salmon
Ⓚ	Fall Salmon
S	Summer Steelhead
Ⓢ	Winter Steelhead
B	Bass
Ⓑ	Striped Bass
P	Perch or Catfish
T	Trout
D	Shad
V	Various Bottomfish
•	Exact Locations

and in the summer, steelhead and salmon. This rocky coastline may be the most scenic stretch in the country. Rte. 101 provides a truly spectacular trip, but don't get so spellbound by the awesome coastline that you forget to ask the fishermen you see what's hitting. And this is the right place to ask him how big they're running, because they do get the really big ones here. If you want a unique experience — take the opportunity of testing the Rogue River's white-water rapids — but only with a guide. Excellent guides love the trip, challenging the turbulent river's falls and shoots. The Rogue's also good from the bank at Agness, Illahe, and Medford. For bassing, the only choice is Lake Selmac, but it's good from either boat or bank.

Southern Oregon is one of the meccas for the young today; and the reason is its wild, remote stretches, coupled with its lack of people. There are gorgeous hikes into national forests or strolls along the Pacific beach. Here's one of the places where the fisherman can cash in on many of the rewards and challenges of the outdoors.

THE SALMON PARTY BOATS

On this lower coast salmon fishermen score heavily from spring to fall, going out on boats from CHARLESTON and COOS BAY. In this region, Oregon's lavish evergreens in rugged, remote mountains form startling backdrops to headwaters of some of the most picturesque and scenic rivers anywhere. Moving south on Rte. 101 to REEDSPORT, you'll hit the UMPQUA RIVER, which rivalled the Rogue River as Zane Grey's favorite. The lower Umpqua produces well year-round for the fisherman on the bank or in a boat. During the summer striped bass as heavy as fifty pounds work the river bottom. This same stretch from REEDSPORT to SCOTTSBURG — is accessible at many points along paralleling Rte. 38 — is also prime water for Chinook and coho salmon, shad, and both summer and winter steelhead. Plug or bait fish for bass, fly fish or spin for shad, and use bait for salmon and steelhead. Ask about guides at REEDS-PORT or WINCHESTER BAY, and you might consider offshore fishing here if the seas aren't running too heavily. A big shad run enters the river in June; and upstream from KELLOGG little fluorescent colored spinners, flies, and jigs are popular with locals. At the junction of the NORTH and SOUTH UMPQUA you can bank fish or wade for winter steelhead and then Chinook salmon in the spring until late June. From summer until Christmas there's terrific steelheading in the North Umpqua. In the STEAMBOAT area, nearly a hundred miles due east of the river's mouth, there's a "flies only" area, and choice riffles and pools await the silent approach of the fly fisherman. Ask at the Steamboat Lodge for directions to the hot pieces of water and fly patterns that are working out. The SOUTH UMPQUA at RIDDLE just off Rte. I-5 is another good place to bank fish for winter steelhead.

NOW FOR THE WINTER STEELHEAD

Just south of Coos Bay at Bandon, the Coquille River flows into the Pacific. The best fishing, particularly for winter

The serenity of North Umpqua River, Oregon.
LOU WIENECKE PHOTO

steelhead, is upstream from BROADBENT to the Siskiyou National Forest boundary. Both the South Fork and the Middle Fork of the Coquille turn hot for steelhead, and bank access is good from the roads that parallel the rivers. Here, the best advice is again to look for concentrations of cars as steelhead move along a river. Near PORT ORFORD, the ELK RIVER is good in the early fall for salmon. It also has winter steelhead, and it's readily accessible at many points inside the Siskiyou National Forest. Pick out your own riffle or pool, though the locals usually can be found where the fish are hitting best. Just a couple of miles from the mouth of the Elk is where the SIXES RIVER runs into the sea. The Sixes is particularly good in the late fall for big Chinook or king salmon of more than thirty-five pounds. About ten miles upriver on the paralleling road Dry Creek comes into the Sixes, and right there is a fine bank fishing spot for winter steelhead.

THE MIGHTY ROGUE

The mighty Rogue River enters the Pacific at Gold Beach. We recommend guided tours of the Rogue, which can be arranged at Gold Beach, WEDDERBURN, and many spots upriver. You'll also find a cannery near Wedderburn where they'll put up your salmon for you. The Rogue is noted for spring and fall salmon runs and for a superb run of winter steelhead. At GRANTS PASS you can arrange a five-day float trip to the river's mouth with proper advance notice. Bank-fishing spots are on the north bank at the mouth of Lobster Creek, on the south side at Kimbell Creek's juncture, at Illahe, and at the mouth of the ILLINOIS RIVER at AGNESS. The waters near Agness are particularly good for yearling steelhead weighing about a half-pound. You can put a boat in there, or you can also find good bank access. Use lures, flies, or salmon eggs. But we don't want to infer that you should restrict your fishing on the Rogue to these spots. This is a long, meandering river with much of its length in national forests where access is no problem. For example, twenty-five miles northwest of GRANTS PASS you might hike the Bureau of Land Management trails westward along the Rogue from the mouth of Grave Creek. Salmon and steelhead run nearly year-round here, but the hiking and fishing is best in spring and fall. Or just north of MEDFORD, at the junction of the ROGUE and Little Butte rivers, you can find good bank fishing. West of Grants Pass at the town of SELMA you'll find a privately owned road paralleling the Illinois, and both rivers are part of Oregon's Scenic Waterways System. Cabins cannot be built without permission from the State Highway Commission. These wild rivers offer good fishing, and as on the Illinois, the owners of cabins are die-hard steelheaders. They know the waters, where the fish are, and what they are hitting. Most are quite hospitable and usually grant fishermen access to the rivers running through or by their property.

For lake fishing, SELMAC LAKE off Rte. 199 at SELMA promises good bass and trout fishing. This lake was designed with the fisherman in mind, and the shoreline seems to wait for sharp-shooting plug casters after largemouth bass.

Nearly at the California border, the CHETCO and WINCHUK RIVERS flow out of the Siskiyou National Forest to the Pacific. At BROOKINGS you can board a saltwater party boat or bank fish for fall salmon on the Chetco. Both rivers have winter steelhead and king salmon for boat fishermen but the only access to the Winchuk is in the National forest. Just to the north, where Rte. 101 crosses Hunter Creek, there's a gravel bar a mile to the west where you can fish or put a boat in. Some other bank fishing access points can be found on upstream and this stretch is especially good for spring Chinook.

KLAMATH BASIN

UPPER KLAMATH LAKE is a huge, sprawling body of water, turning marshy in its northern end. It is, to many a fisherman's way of thinking, a supreme lake for rainbow trout. Here they go to sixteen pounds, and the majority easily top three pounds. If it's the fight and test of a lunker rainbow you want, this is your lake. KLAMATH FALLS and Pelican Bay are two of the hotter spots where there's excellent access and boats to be rented. In the spring and fall, the big ones hit best, though you can get them year-round if you troll. (It's closed north of Modoc Point after October 31.) Shore fishing is also excellent when they're biting, both on the UPPER KLAMATH and its feeder river, the WILLIAMSON. This beautiful river is the home of the lake rainbow, and its lower reaches are good boat water. Again, the trout get up to fifteen pounds. South of CHILO-QUIN, where Rte. 97 crosses the Williamson, take the Day School Road south to a fine resort with a trailer court. North of Chiloquin there's a good camping area where no boats are allowed. About here the river starts working into more isolated country, and it's good hiking terrain.

South and west of the Upper Klamath are a number of fine lakes that offer a variety of experiences. Nearby LAKE OF THE WOODS (on Rte. 140) has a resort and also caters to the "long john" crowd in the winter. The ice fishing can be fast and fun. Then about two miles west on Rte. 140 and just east of Fish Lake, turn north for a few miles to FOUR MILE LAKE. This is a high, remote lake nestled among the lush evergreens and scenic peaks of the Cascade Mountains. It holds a nice variety of trout and salmon, which hit best in the spring and fall. The lake is right on the hikers' Skyline Trail and it's just forty-five miles north to CRATER LAKE. We don't mean to infer it's that easy a stroll, and we'd recommend picking up detailed topographical maps before striking out. All of this country is terrific for camping out, and there are superb small streams and lakes you can hike to.

Southwest of this region, toward Medford, more easily reached off Rtes. I-5 and 66, lie two more bodies of water surrounded by evergreens and full of trout. HOWARD PRAIRIE and HYATT reservoirs are good in August and September, and resorts make them a nice vacation spot.

East from Klamath Falls the irrigation canals provide a lot of truly localized fishing and the spots shift and change; and if you want to try them, we'd recommend you talk with the local anglers or the fishermen in the sporting goods stores. LOST RIVER, for a fifteen-mile stretch between Olene and Bonanza is certainly no slouch when it comes to big bass production. A seven-pound river bass is a tough customer, and you can get at them along here either from a boat or from the bank. Another twenty-five miles east of BONANZA (on Rte. 140) and south of Bly, there's a good Bureau of Land Management campground at GERBER RESERVOIR. A boat is recommended, and the warm-water species such as bass and crappie are most active in the spring and fall. About twenty-five miles northeast of Bly, though you'll have to drive three times as far and much of it over unimproved roads, are two scenic, "chockful-of-trout" lakes in the shadow of 8,390-foot Gearhart Mountain. CAMP-BELL and DEADHORSE are small, but they usually produce well as the fishing pressure on them is not great. Farther east on Rte. 140 to LAKEVIEW and you'll find some superb, stocked trout on Camas Creek and Deep Creek right off the highway. North of the highway, Priday Reservoir produces rainbow that are partial to bait.

CENTRAL LAKES

On the west slope of the Cascades you'll see some of the most gorgeous, lush country anywhere. Fast, free-flowing streams form in the high country and rollick toward the Pacific. Here lie sparkling clear, unmatched Crater Lake, the headwaters of the Deschutes River, and numerous sylvan lakes. The Deschutes first pours over huge, sculptured rocks in the west. Southwest of Bend is Lava Lake, which for years has been called the headwaters of the Deschutes; but now an Oregonian, Bruce Estes, is attempting to prove that Elk Lake, to the north of Lava Lake, is the source. The only connection between the river and the two lakes — if one indeed exists — would be through underground channels. On the east slope, well, you'll find some good fishing, besides some fine sand dunes, lava beds, and picturesque butte country.

Starting in the southeast off Rte. 31 — you'll see the access roads easily enough — good trout fishing can be found in THOMPSON VALLEY RESERVOIR and the tiny Ana Reservoir.

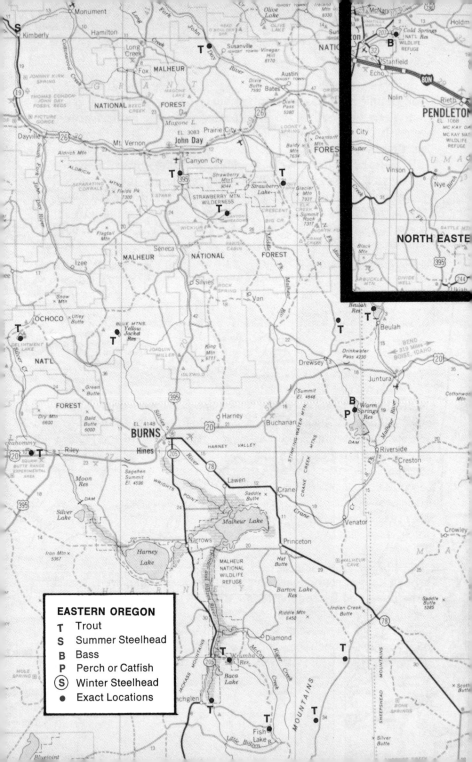

EASTERN OREGON

T	Trout
S	Summer Steelhead
B	Bass
P	Perch or Catfish
Ⓢ	Winter Steelhead
•	Exact Locations

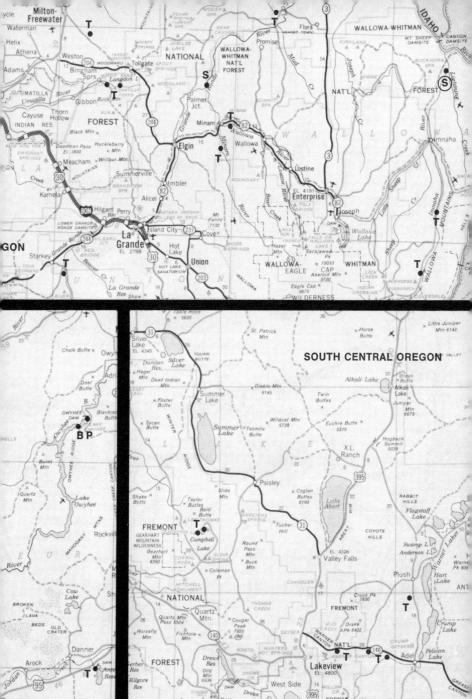

Directly north of Upper Klamath Lake, CRATER LAKE is one of nature's grandest spots, the sheer walls of the volcanic crater rising into fresh green beauty, but if you want a trout you'll have to approach these perfectly clear waters on your stomach. Popular DIAMOND LAKE yields the best early summer limits of one- to three-pound trout for the fisherman using flies, flatfish, and cheese. Except for July and August when the algae blooms, the water is delightfully blue-green and the fish flavorful. Farther north, ODELL and CRESCENT lakes (on Rte. 58) are superb in the spring with Crescent standing up better through the summer. Twenty-pound lake trout lurk in both lakes, as do all kinds of small, game Kokanee. Resorts, campgrounds, and boats are available. To the northeast on DAVIS LAKE, fly fishermen with their own boats take very big rainbows and landlocked salmon. The salmon get up to five pounds in this relatively shallow water. There's a campground and a paved boat ramp on the south side. In the same area, some of the prettiest lake country in the state lies in the Willamette National Forest. WALDO LAKE off Rte. 58 is a standout summer lake with good rainbow and brook trout in its many bays. You should try bait at medium depths. Lava Lake usually will enable you to catch a limit of twelve- to sixteen-inch trout in the spring and fall. The shorelines are densely forested and the setting is superb for hooking into one of the big brookies. The fish go deep during the hot months.

Go east through BEND to PRINEVILLE and you'll find OCHOCO LAKE (return to the northeastern map), where excellent facilities and lots of trout to twenty inches make it a family favorite. South at the PRINEVILLE RESERVOIR, fishermen go for trout and both largemouth and smallmouth bass, the bass weighing as much as five pounds. The lake is good year-round, and it's fine for vacationing fishermen. The upper end is best, from Jasper Point northeast. The bass dwell under rimrocks, lying in wait for forage fish and insects. And while you are here, you should check out CROOKED RIVER, which is good fly fishing and spinning for big trout if the water is not too turbid.

The river is readily accessible from the road, and big rainbows to fifteen pounds lurk in its pools.

Just to the northwest of Rte. 20 at CAMP SHERMAN, near the MOUNT JEFFERSON WILDERNESS, the facilities are great with nice cabins, wooded campgrounds, horseback riding, guided pack trips, and, of course, great rainbow fishing on the METOLIUS RIVER. It's good all season, especially for fly fishermen. Wooley worms and nymphs work best in the pools and eddies. Farther northwest, DETROIT LAKE holds good populations of trout and Kokanee. It's a fluctuating reservoir, and the river arms pay off best, particularly for slow trollers using spoons and flatfish. Some bank fishing areas along the south and east shores are good for bait fishing with worms or cheese. The state park provides about two hundred good campsites, plenty of picnic tables, a boat launch, and a fine swimming area.

Running north to the Columbia, the DESCHUTES RIVER has not been developed well for fishermen because it flows through canyons, private land, and Indian reservations. An exception is at the SHERARS BRIDGE, an historic stagecoach stop on the Oregon Trail, where a fine BLM (U.S. Bureau of Land Management) project has resulted in a popular, if overcrowded, shoreline camping and fishing area. May, June, and September are good months for salmon fishing above the bridge. August and September are best for steelhead below the bridge. We should warn you, however, the temperature is likely to hit a hundred degrees in the summer. Just south of 11,235-foot MOUNT HOOD, high in a national forest, nestles scenic TIMOTHY LAKE. No resorts are there, but it has excellent camping and boat launching. It's a good family spot with the Kokanee, rainbows, and native trout usually biting well and often.

THE HIGH DESERT

The High Desert is a bizarre land, rugged and wearing as only desert can be. In the summer it's hot, really hot, dry, and fertile — where there's water. In the winter it gets truly cold, a biting wind whipping off sheer buttes and over lava beds and volcanic craters. The stark beauty here resembles a fantasy land at times where the erosion of time has sculptured weird formations in rock. Dry Harney Lake is a maze of limbs and roots of birch trees — all petrified.

The best fishing in this southeastern quarter is in man-made reservoirs where trout grow to six pounds in two or three years — that's twice as fast as on such beautiful, scenic streams as the Rogue and Umpqua — and bass and crappie mature into big, wily specimens.

On Oregon's eastern border, southwest of Jordan Valley just off Rte. 95, ANTELOPE RESERVOIR is prime water for big rainbow trout throughout the year. There's a boat launch on the west side, but bank fishing with bait — worms are popular — into the murky waters is exceptionally good. Just to the north of Jordan Valley lies the 55-mile-long OWYHEE LAKE. To get there, you should head up to Vale on Rte. 20 and drive south, or hit it from the east via Rtes. 95 and 20. Drive past the dam

A view of Deschutes River, Oregon.
LOU WIENECKE PHOTO

to the state park where the facilities are superb for family camping and bank fishing. Owyhee is one of the best crappie lakes in the west, though it's also good for bass and catfish. Jigs and spinners are popular, but bait probably works better. It's good fishing year-round, but it's phenomenal in the spring.

Moving west along Rte. 20 to JUNTURA, check for current fishing reports regarding BEULAH, WARM SPRINGS, and MALHEUR RESERVOIRS. Pick the one that's hot. All three excite the local fishermen in the spring and early summer. Beulah comes through again in October, and you could try your hand at ice fishing there for rainbow trout. Warm Springs supports both largemouth and smallmouth bass, and they can get rowdy. The north end is usually best and its waters seem ideal for plugs.

LAKE FISHING FOR RAINBOW

Some excellent rainbow trout fishing surrounds BURNS, which is another sixty miles west on Rte. 20. To the southeast of Burns, Juniper and Mann Lakes offer good cutthroats and rainbows, but they are remote and the roads in are not all-weather. If the weather reports are favorable, these lakes offer good wading and you can get a small boat in easily. The cooler months are best. Further south on Rte. 205 near FRENCH-GLEN, FISH and KRUMBO LAKES vie with the BLITZEN RIVER for the best rainbow fishing. No motors are allowed on either lake, though easy access satisfies most fishermen, especially at Fish Lake. (There is a river in Harney County named the "DONNER UND BLITZEN RIVER," German for thunder and lightning. It was named during the Snake War of 1864 when troops under the command of George B. Currey crossed it during a thunderstorm. Locally, the river is called simply Blitzen.)

North of BURNS in the Malheur National Forest, DELINT-MENT and YELLOWJACKET LAKES offer excellent trout scaling in at over five pounds. The roads are fine, but you should head up to Delintment from RILEY. Another few miles west of Riley puts you at the CHICAHOMINY LAKE right on Rte. 20. This is a good trout lake, best in cool months, though ice fishing is popular too. The campgrounds and boat launch are fairly good.

THE REMOTE NORTHEAST

This is great country for exploring. There aren't many people around, though it's country with the grandeur we expect out of the best of the west: remote canyons and rock mesas, the valley of the old Oregon Trail, the Snake River gorge where Hell's Canyon divides Oregon and Idaho. Gold in the north fork of the John Day River drew many miners in the late nineteenth century.Old ghost towns and caved-in mines are fun to poke into, but there's little to match the fascination of trying to pan a couple of small nuggets or slivers of gold out of the river. Heavily forested slopes leading to snow-capped mountains cover the eastern border country. Deep in the Wallowa-Whitman National Forest the Matterhorn and Sacajawea Peaks rise to more than 10,000 feet.

THE JOHN DAY RIVER

Moving south, the John Day River at KIMBERLY is popular for winter runs of steelhead. Farther upriver, near the town of JOHN DAY (on Rte. 26), an abundance of trout can be caught when the river is up in May and June. The stream, however, cuts through mostly private land, and you will have to ask permission to gain access. The best stretch goes from MOUNT VERNON through PRAIRIE CITY and on to TROUT FARM CAMP, which is public. In this same section, Canyon Creek and CANYON MEADOWS LAKE are stocked with rainbow, and these waters hold up quite well through the summer months. The MIDDLE FORK JOHN DAY from BATES northwest to Rte. 395 is paralleled by a good, improved mountain road and it holds good nine- to fourteen-inch rainbows. And the North Fork John Day, accessible easily only where it's crossed by Rte. 395 at Dale, provides good summer trout fishing. The ranger station at Dale is a good stop to check for specific directions and camping locations.

HIKING THE UMATILLA

The PENDLETON area's best fishing is east of GIBBON in the UMATILLA RIVER's North and South forks during May and June. Umatilla is an Indian word meaning "water rippling over sand," and it even SOUNDS like the fish should be there. At road's end east of Gibbon, you can hike from the corporation guard station on to Coyote Creek and pick up rainbows and an occasional Dolly Varden. McKAY RESERVOIR sparkles in the spring and early summer for the bass fisherman. A rough boat launch is at the upper end. Another car-top boat lake northwest of PENDLETON, COLD SPRINGS RESERVOIR, features wade fishing for bass and crappie in April and May when the water is clear. In the South Fork Walla Walla River southeast of MILTON-FREEWATER, some nice rainbows go for worms and cheese bait.

The MINAM RIVER is best in August and September for fly fishing for rainbow trout, though you'll need to make some short to medium hikes in. Take Rte. 82 three miles south of the town of MINAM, turn along Rte. 110, and go upstream from where the road approaches this clear, tinkling stream. East of Minam on Rte. 82 a more accessible area for trout is on the WALLOWA RIVER. North of Minam, October and November are the best months to put in a small river boat on the GRANDE RONDE RIVER at Rondowa. You can make a two-day float trip north for steelhead and occasionally spot some big bull elk on the banks. This trip can be adventuresome; take your boat out at Troy. And at Troy, a good summer hike in to the WENAHA RIVER for trout can be arranged so that you'll have reserved cabins waiting.

THE ROARING SNAKE RIVER

Over near the Idaho border, the Imnaha River — north of the town of IMNAHA — supports a good run of steelhead from late September through the winter. The Cow Creek Bridge is popular and some fishermen hike north toward the Idaho border, often catching five- to seven-pound steelies. South of Imnaha, the river is consistently good for rainbows through the summer and fall. Just to the east of the Imnaha River and paralleling it, runs the Grand Canyon of the SNAKE RIVER, or Hells Canyon as most folks call it. This is excellent fishing during the fall and winter for both bass and steelhead. It's a treacherous river, of course, and guided boat trips out of Lewiston, Idaho, or at Oxbow Dam in Oregon are necessary. From Oxbow a guide will take parties into the scenic canyon, and it gets tough — understandably — to concentrate on fishing in this turbulent, beautiful canyon.

NEVADA

The action in Nevada is fast, and we're not talking about what you'll find in the casinos. The fishing is terrific — once you find some water. Lake Mead, one of the huge reservoirs sprawling along the Colorado River, lies only thirty minutes outside of Las Vegas, a fine counter-experience to the garish glitter and neon night life. The lake promises some of the best bass fishing in the West. Up north, Pyramid Lake, a large natural lake just south of the high steppes called the Smoke Creek Desert and forty-five minutes north of Reno, holds tremendous trout. Here in Nevada, you must look beyond the hot sands and lizards to find the lakes, trout streams, and beaver ponds. The State Fish and Game Department stocks its waters heavily. But perhaps because of Nevada's hot, dry image, the state doesn't lure its share of traveling fishermen. State fishery officials have complained in the past that some sections of water are neglected, and that the trout with their short life span die more often of old age than from angling pressure.

In a way it's fitting that the best fishing in this big state is for big fish in big lakes — Lake Mead, Lake Mohave, Walker Lake,

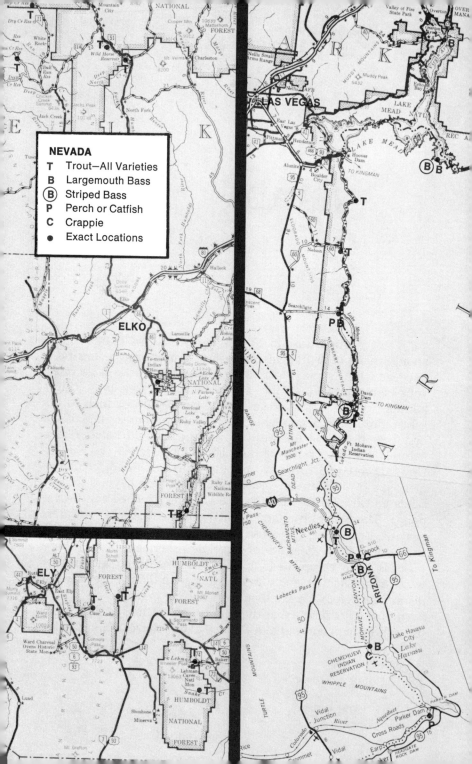

NEVADA

T	Trout—All Varieties
B	Largemouth Bass
Ⓑ	Striped Bass
P	Perch or Catfish
C	Crappie
●	Exact Locations

Pyramid Lake and, of course, Lake Tahoe. Each of these beautiful lakes has its own charm, unique grandeur, and trophy-sized fish. They provide a full experience for the fisherman. They offer consistent action, the promise of a stringer of pan-size fish while affording the excellent chance for the always-sought-after "big one."

THE HUGE COLORADO RESERVOIRS

Starting in southern Nevada, the fisherman can find miles of superb fishing waters along the winding route of the Colorado River. Most of these spots are within a couple of hours drive from LAS VEGAS. Nearly at the southernmost tip of the state is Davis Dam, which forms meandering LAKE MOHAVE. Five miles below the dam on the Arizona side of the Colorado River you can rent boats or fish from the bank near Bullhead City. From March to July striped bass that weigh as much as forty pounds strike sardines, water dogs, and other baits, particularly at night. And during the day, the trout fishing is worthwhile.

In Lake Mohave, you might go after the big rainbow that prowl the lake waters. They go well over fifteen pounds, and they fall for trolled flatfish, drifted cheese, and nightcrawlers. Your best chances for these huge trout occur from August through November and in a stretch of water east of NELSON running from five miles below to five miles above Eldorado Canyon. This is where a "front" occurs, where the cold current flowing south collides with the warmer waters of the lake. Bait fish school up in the front, and curiously the trout find this situation tantalizing. Rental boats are available.

Two spots in Mohave are especially good for largemouth bass and catfish in the spring, early summer, and fall: Cottonwood Cove east of SEARCHLIGHT and Willow Beach south of Hoover Dam. You must drive to Arizona and twenty miles southeast after crossing the dam to reach Willow Beach, where there is a boat launch and good bank fishing. This area is good the year-round for trout.

A BASS BONANZA

Above Hoover Dam and east of Las Vegas sprawls huge LAKE MEAD with its great largemouth bass fishing. It isn't as "hot" as it was some years ago when it was nationally famed for record-size bass, but it's still the place to take a limit of bass weighing up to six pounds each. These days, however, you usually must fish quite deep, say twenty-five feet, to get the big fellows. Efforts have been successful, though, in stabilizing the water level during spawning season; the hatch of bass has improved and so, naturally, has the fishing. Striped bass, too, have been doing well in Mead and you've always the shot at a twenty- to twenty-five-pounder. The Overton Beach boat landing south of Glendale rents boats, but for slightly better bassing and striper action go some sixth miles from HOOVER DAM on the Arizona side to Temple Bar. Boats are available as are all other facilities, such as a trailer camp, campground, restaurant, and air strip.

Lakes Mead and Mohave are prolific breeding grounds for bass. The only place a fisherman will find better bass fishing in the far West is up north in Washington in the Potholes. Bass fishing is great sport, one wc recommend. Because of the bass' liking for shorelines, logs, and lily pads, he is an ideal target for plug casters who like to toss lures at the most likely spots. Unfortunately, most of the year big bass dwell down near the bottom where the cooler temperatures are more suited to them. Then, fishing for them becomes difficult, and only the fisherman skilled with lead-headed lures or minnows has a good chance of hooking one. Here in Nevada, you'll find mostly largemouths because they do so well in the huge lakes. It's the smallmouth that likes the moving water of clear streams. Where the largemouth is black and white, the smallmouth is brownish. He is a long-winded fighter and likes to jump and break water more than the largemouth. Preferring smaller lures, the smallmouth is more picky about striking your lure and is harder for the beginning bass fisherman to hook. Bass fishing is the sport across the southern half of the country, and the estimated six million bass fishermen may have replaced — or are getting ready to replace — the trout fishermen as the most eager, dedicated, and devoted troop of anglers. The building of so many huge dams in the past decade or two, creating big reservoirs, has opened up tremendous new fishing opportunities for bass. But few lakes have stood up as well as Mead and Mohave over the years. After four or five years most lakes are no longer considered hot and level off with a bass population something less than what inspires and excites the true bass fisherman. But these two lakes have persisted, and now the bass are jumping again and in good numbers.

THE BEAUTY OF LAKE MEAD

The day we ventured out on Lake Mead it was sunny, clear, and very hot. We wanted to look at Hoover Dam and get a good impression of Mead's size, so we drove across the dam and into Arizona, renting a boat at Temple Bar. This is dry desert land, but along the shoreline you find fingers of the lake with good vegetation. About a 30-minute boat run north of the marina we turned into a finger that looked promising. The water there is clear, shimmering, and we drifted on it quietly, casting in near to brush and vegetation. We wanted a big bass, but we really were after action — any action at all after two days in Las Vegas.

It doesn't matter whether you are in Oklahoma, Florida, or Nevada, when that first bass of the day hits your plug you know the thrill of tangling with a game, fighting fish. The bass is only dainty when he's sniffing out a lure — once he takes it, you've a fine battle. As in all freshwater fishing, you need the proper gear, the right strength line, and the proper rod to fully enjoy your fish. But as any bass fisherman knows, the key to success is to know the waters of a lake, to know where the lunkers like to roam, and where the smaller ones like to feed. We didn't, but after an hour we had two bass, each weighing nearly two pounds. By then the sun was boring down, and the water was too inviting. It was a great swim, all the better because of the sharp contrast of clear, cool water with the sunbaked hills and rough bluffs surrounding the lake.

SPARKLING LAKE TAHOE

Up near RENO lie Tahoe and Pyramid lakes. Though Lake Tahoe sports some huge lake trout, they are tough to find, and you'll have a more pleasant afternoon if you content yourself with drinking in the beauty of this alpine retreat. Nestled high in the Sierra Nevada Mountains, its strikingly blue, clear waters reflect the snow caps and lush evergreen forests. In the spring, drive south along the lake's shoreline on Rte. 28 out of IN-CLINE VILLAGE until you see boulders protruding out of the water. Park the car, arm yourself with a small spoon or worms, and cast out from shore for trout or Kokanee salmon. There is a boat launch at Cave Rock by Zephyr Cove, and just to the south at Nevada Beach there is overnight camping. On the other side of Reno, LAHONTAN RESERVOIR supports a good spring fishery for white bass. They'll get as big as two pounds and like to hit spoons and plugs.

THE HOME OF WORLD-RECORD TROUT

If you get near Reno, however, and you are interested in fishing one of the finest light-tackle trout lakes in the country, you have only to drive thirty-three miles north of Reno (on Rte. 33) to the town of SUTCLIFFE. There, fishermen have access to PYRAMID LAKE, a surrealistic scene where spiraling pinnacles rise out of the lake and sheer, rugged bluffs seem to hang over the water. Here is where the big Lahontan cutthroat trout rise to grab shallow-running flies and spoons from November through March. Right at Sutcliffe and up the lake to Pelican Point, four to ten pounders are caught by both boat and bank fishermen. You can get more information on precisely where the trout are and what they're hitting from Al or Ann at the Sutcliffe Bar. Remember, though, that during the one hundred-degree summer months the only action will be from Sacramento perch. The State Fish and Game Information officer in Reno says it isn't really so hot. But, he adds with a smile, "the horny toads carry around sticks for shade." There are not, to be sure, any trees; only the stark, barren pinnacles.

The day I went out on Pyramid, it was clear and the tang of fall was in the air. We were motoring across the lake and the steady sputter of the outboard lulled me into a reverie. I was thinking of the lake's heyday, which had been the first part of the 1900s. Pyramid must have looked much the same then as it does now except its level was some eighty feet higher. There is a lesson here: The changes in this lake over the years are a prime example of how a body of water can be ruined, forgotten, and then finally restored through thoughtful water and fishing management programs.

The scene in those days is hardly imaginable: Paiute Indians working their nets in and above the lake at the mouth of the Truckee River, lifting hordes of yard-long fish onto the shore. Records show that one year the Paiutes shipped over a hundred tons to markets as far east as Chicago. Records also show that in 1925 Paiute Johnny Skimmerhorn caught the world's record cutthroat in Pyramid, a forty-one pounder. It was just another big fish to him, but the feat lured movie stars, a U.S. President,

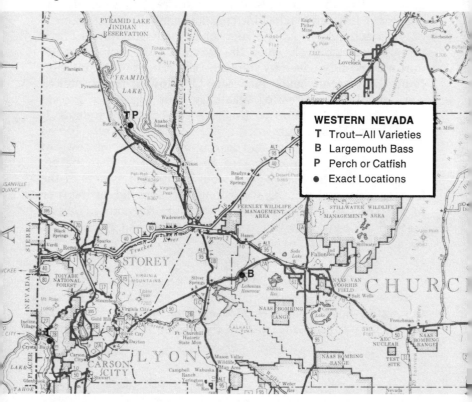

and dignitaries from many parts of the world to fish Pyramid. But then Pyramid was already dying. In 1906 a poorly designed diversionary dam had been built on the Truckee, and because this river was the lake's only source of water and spawning grounds for its trout, the great lake's fish first declined, then disappeared. The super strain of cutthroat was gone forever; and the Indians, promised protection by treaty, were left without their commercial fishery. Man had failed to control "progress."

Finally, in 1950, with the establishment of the Nevada Fish and Game Commission, steps were taken to restore Pyramid's great fishery. Biologists introduced a strain of Lahontan cutthroat and later hybrids of rainbow and cutthroat which could thrive in its rich but alkaline water. Though not as long-lived as the native strain, these fish fight hard and grow rapidly. One biologist dubbed Pyramid the most fertile lake he has ever seen. Whereas in two years California's Berryessa and Eagle Lakes grow trout to three pounds, Pyramid grows them to eight! The number of fish now trucked into the lake annually for stocking is only a fraction of what the lake can actually support. A bright promise came, though, when the Pyramid Lake Task Force Report was recently issued by the U.S. Department of the Interior. It not only recommends increasing the flow of fresh water to stem the lake's increasing alkalinity, but suggests a project which would be a boon to fishermen and resident Indians. It would rework the mouth of the Truckee River and establish an Indian-managed spawning and rearing facility near the town of Nixon. The fishing potential of the lake might then be approached, and the real benefit would go to the owners of the lake, the Pyramid Paiutes. But enough background, as the flow of the Truckee into Pyramid is now before the courts. We had reached Pelican Point where my companion and guide, Reno fireman Joe Granata, expected action.

THE LAHONTAN TROUT IN ACTION

He was trolling a spoon, and before I could get my rig into the water, he was muttering, "Got one." He had kicked the motor into neutral and was slowly reeling in when a slender silver and pink missile broke the water. "She's a keeper," Joe enthused. Anywhere else a "keeper" trout is usually ten or twelve inches, but here it's got to be at least nineteen. After a couple of stout runs the trout headed for the boat and nose-dived into the net.

We were using fourteen-pound test line; that's heavy for nine-teen-inchers but necessary for the big ones here, which often get close to twenty pounds. We were trolling just beyond the reach of two fly fishermen on the bank. "They get big ones on flies here," Joe said. "Each year the magazine contests show several fly fishing prizewinners from Pyramid."

Just then my hook snagged on a log — a live log. My rod hairpinned and the line screamed off. Joe had lost two big ones last year before netting a thirteen-pounder, and he was worried I'd lose this one. The first time the fish ran toward us, Joe missed him with the net. The trout looked huge as it swerved beneath the boat. Keeping a tight line, I again worked him in close; and as Joe was getting the net ready, my fish suddenly spit out the hook. Joe made a scoop with the net, some-how trapping him against the boat. I had an eight-pounder, one of the nicest trout I've ever hooked. It was a memorable day; Pyramid is one of those places that puts its imprint on you. Indeed, it seems to demand recognition these days, since offi-cials, fishermen, and Indians truly want to restore Pyramid to what it once was — which doesn't mean the fishing is bad now. But Pyramid could again be the best trout-fishing lake in the country. Today it is only one of the best.

THE TROUT OF EASTERN NEVADA

On the other side of Nevada, along Rte. 50, are a few summer trout-fishing streams. If you head due west out of BAKER, practically on the eastern border, you'll hit two campgrounds, one on LEHMAN CREEK and the other on Baker Creek. Both have rainbow trout averaging seven or eight inches in length, with the largest about twelve. For slightly larger fish, including the wily brown trout, move south to SNAKE CREEK. About six miles southeast of Baker, take the road that branches west off Rte. 73. The road parallels much of the stream, and ten miles up you'll find two campgrounds.

Over in the HUMBOLDT NATIONAL FOREST, some of the more primitive country delights fly rod purists after trout. Head west of Baker for thirty-two miles on Rte. 50 — and two miles before the junction with Rte. 93 — turn north along the Schell Creek Range. Eight small creeks meander down the mountainsides and disappear in the sand. Though these creeks may be only five miles long and only three feet wide in spots, they hold a good population of eight-inch trout, with some going twice that length. The most southerly of these brooks, CLEVE CREEK, has a nice campground. On the western edge of the national forest, Cave Creek Reservoir and CAVE LAKE are especially good for the fisherman with the car-top boat. To reach these trout, take the road north off Rte. 50, which is about seven miles southeast of Ely.

Or you can hit another fine spot on the other side of Ely. Drive southwest on Rte. 6, turning southeast on Rte. 38 to Sunnyside. You can camp in the Kirch Wildlife area and then put a boat into the ADAMS-McGILL RESERVOIR. The bank fishing is excellent for trout to four pounds and bass to three pounds.

In the center of the state, about thirty miles south of Rte. 50 just off of Rte. 8A, lies Groves Lake in the TOIYABE NATIONAL FOREST. It holds brown trout that weigh as much as eight pounds, and it's good fishing from the bank with bait, lures, or flies. Turn south off Rte. 8A on Kingston Creek Road which leads to a campground at the lake. There are a number of turnoffs from Rte. 8A, and nearly all of them take you to small streams with catchable-sized trout.

SIDE TRIPS OFF ROUTE I-80

There are some good fishing holes off Rte. I-80, too. RUBY LAKE lies south of Elko off Rte. 46, but it's a rough drive over high Harrison Pass. We recommend cutting down from WELLS via Rte. 93. It's more of a mammoth duck marsh than a lake, but it has rainbows up to seventeen pounds and many small largemouth bass. The best fishing, particularly for trout, is during the first part of May and again in September. The bass hit all summer, and limits of twenty largemouth aren't uncommon, if you use poppers, spinners, or flies. The campgrounds at Ruby Lake are exceptional. North of the lake — twenty miles south of ELKO on Rte. 46 — is the South Fork of the HUMBOLDT RIVER, a fine, bubbling stream on the Te-Moak Indian Reservation. You need to ask for permission to fish the Humboldt, but it's worth the asking as twenty-inch rainbows will hit on bait or flies.

ON THE NORTHERN BORDER

Up north near the Idaho border, Wild Horse Reservoir makes for superb family fun. It's seventy-five miles north on Rte. 51, turning off Rte. I-80 at Elko. The rainbow run to eighteen inches in length and will hit anything from marshmallows to lures or flies. The fishing off the bank is excellent. Campgrounds are at the reservoir and a couple of miles farther up Rte. 51 along the OWYHEE RIVER. About forty miles to the west, the adventurous can work their way back to WILSON CREEK and SHEEP CREEK RESERVOIRS. These are best during the spring, early summer, and fall. The last stretch of the roads are unpaved, but they should be no problem.

WASHINGTON

The silver salmon were running in the mouth of the Columbia River, and for the past few days they had been nice ones — ten to fifteen pounds. Up here, salmon fishing rivals steelhead fishing for glamor status, and most of these fishermen on the party boats live in these parts. Our charter boat had beat through a stiff Pacific chop after clearing the Ilwaco breakwater. At 5:45 A.M. I had joined about seventy-five other fishermen in the still pitch-dark morning to climb on the party boats; and now with a queasy feeling from the boat's ridiculously uneven roll, I wondered if silver (or coho) salmon fishing was worth the effort.

But within minutes of dropping my first bait into the Pacific, I understood the salmon's popularity. The salmon slaps the herring first, then takes it in one gulp, setting the hook. This first silver was a nice one, and on his initial flight he was zinging the line off my reel. Salmon are spectacular fighters and this one was no exception. He would leap clear of the water to dance on his tail for long seconds — seemingly trying to spit the hook back in my face. I was reminded of similar antics by striped marlin, but salmon of course do not have that kind of size, strength, or dash. But they have heart and it was a good five-minutes struggle bringing him in near the boat. Just then he swerved, diving beneath the boat. That proved to be the hairy time as it's a little difficult working your way aft on a party boat with another dozen fishermen alongside, all with lines in the water. At the fantail, I had him — flashing silver several feet beneath the water — in front of me. He was the best of my limit of three for the day, a fifteen-pounder. The captain of the boat said that day was not unusual, even though all of the fishermen on board had limits shortly after lunchtime. Salmon fishing does not provide the back-breaking struggle that comes with huge ocean fish, but it does provide the same kind of dash, flash, and action. The salmon is a worthy fish, and more so because he's such fine eating.

ALL KINDS OF ACTION

Here in Washington, this is the action that thrills fishermen. The waters don't have fish "so thick you could walk across the broad Columbia," as Lewis and Clark reported in 1805, but still the fishing is among the best anywhere. The celebrated fishing is for salmon and steelhead trout, which often go twenty to twenty-five pounds. Of the two salmon found most frequently in these parts, the king (or Chinook) can weigh up to eighty pounds while the silver seldom top twenty pounds. The salmon run in the Columbia the whole year, but the fishing is fastest when silvers arrive for their annual dash to spawn upriver in August and September. The king's run starts in April. The steelhead makes his four-month winter run starting in November. The winter steelhead can be found all along the western slopes of the Olympic and Cascade ranges, but the finest streams are to the north, feeding into the Puget Sound.

These Cascade and Olympic mountain streams also offer excellent trout fishing, especially for rainbow, native cutthroat, and dolly varden. There are also salmon in the glacier-fed streams running down the Olympics to the Pacific. Certain rivers are better than others, and a few should, in fact, be forgotten. It may take an hour longer to reach some of the spots we will describe, but our aim is to put you into good fishing areas — and not just on the most convenient stretch of water.

Washington is the prime example of big country in the west where terrain can quickly move from arid desert to high mountain country to broad coastal plains, all within a couple of hundred miles. For the purist, the fisherman who longs to hold his own silent reverie with nature, there are quiet stretches high in both the Olympic and Cascade ranges where few others venture and the Game Department officials have no cause to stock some of these fast-flowing streams. Or for the unique breeds of fishermen who are partial only to flies or who wish to pursue the wily bass, they have their spots. Fly fishing is particularly good in the free-flowing streams on the eastern slope of the Cascades while the best bass waters lie in the eastern and southern parts of the state.

Salmon fishing requires no license in either fresh or salt water, but it is essential to check state regulations on seasons, size limits, and prohibited areas before wetting a hook. For trout, a license costs a nonresident six dollars for a week, plus two dollars if you go after steelhead. Be sure to pick up the state fishing pamphlet at an information station or at a sporting goods store when entering the state. It is extremely helpful and includes the telephone numbers of the Game Department's ten regional offices who welcome your telephone calls about water conditions and favored locations.

THE WONDROUS OLYMPIC PENINSULA

Fishing is, of course, much more than the action and the battle to land the trophy or fill the pan. And for those other pleasures, Washington is equally superb. The day after we had thrilled to the salmon, we headed north into the Olympic Peninsula. We had heard much about the densely vegetated rain forests, the towering spruce and fir, the wide, white sand of the ocean beaches.

And of the mighty Hoh River. The majestic river flows from

headwaters high up in the Olympic glacier fields. We crossed it at Route 101 and turned to follow its north bank to the Pacific, along a dirt road marked with a sign to Oil City. We climbed slowly to the peak of the coastal hills and suddenly had one of those awesome views, more the exciting for its unexpectedness. For long minutes we looked across broad valleys of huge trees and the slicing silver ribbon of the Hoh. At the base of the descent we saw wheel tracks leading toward the river; they stopped just short of a glade perched a few feet above the fast-moving river, which curved away, forming a fine, deep fishing hole. For a long hour we had no luck, and by then the women had the water paints out. The rest of the afternoon we lounged on the grass, painting small rocks with faces, flowers, and fish. Delightful . . . the sun was warm, and a quick dip and a beer made it one of those afternoons long remembered. But the Hoh wasn't giving up its fish this day. And the reason was because it had turned exceptionally warm, and the milky white flow of water off the glaciers had discolored the stream.

This huge chunk of land jutting up between the Pacific and the Puget Sound startles travelers from back East with its remote isolation. Natives call it the last wilderness and with reason. The sparse population lives on the coastal flats, leaving the OLYMPIC NATIONAL PARK's rain forest and snow-capped peaks for the wide-eyed visitor. Yet, these unique sights are easily reached. The walk through the rain forest's Hall of Mosses is a pleasant twenty-minute hike from the park headquarters, which lies on the free-flowing, glacier-fed HOH RIVER. Or, you can drive up to mile-high Hurricane Ridge where the stark whiteness of the mountains contrasts grandly with the evergreen stands surging up the steep slopes.

The trout and salmon fishing matches the wild countryside. The rivers have romantic Indian names — the Bogachiel, Soleduck, Humptulips, Queets, Quinault — and the fishing in them is terrific. Most of the rivers are fed by glaciers, so when a warm spell hits they turn milky from the runoff and the fish simply refuse to bite. But the rest of the time, well, you'll have good success getting sea-run cutthroat trout, Dolly Varden, steelhead, and all sizes of jack and adult salmon.

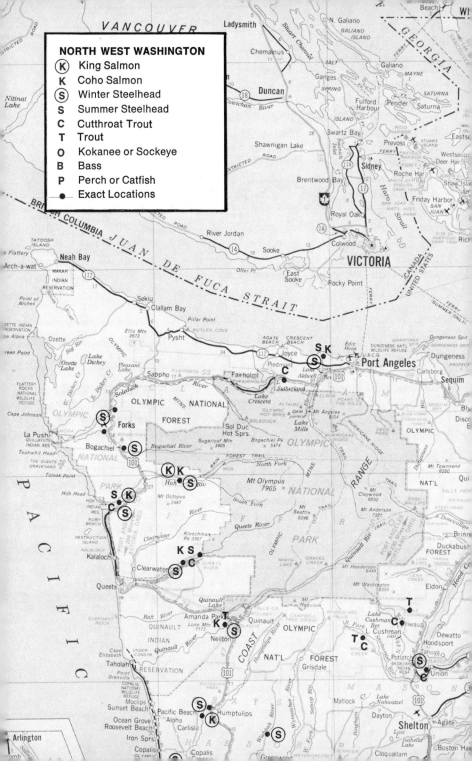

Knowledgeable guides increase a fisherman's chances immensely, of course, and knowledgeable Indian guides on a superb river in an Indian reservation increase a fisherman's chances immeasurably. The Quinault Indians offer trips on their QUINAULT RIVER in a dugout canoe at the height of steelhead season in December. They know the river, naturally enough, and they know steelhead. Climb in a dugout with an Indian guide and you have a unique experience ahead, and often one full of good fishing. Telephone the Quinault Lodge for trip information.

SALMON AND STEELHEAD

Heading north into the peninsula on U.S. 101 takes you first to Grays Harbor. Rather than trying the first stream you cross, we recommend that you stick with the HUMPTULIPS RIVER, which is the Olympic Peninsula's best for salmon and steelhead. Though the river is good for sea-run cutthroat and smaller jack salmon to about three pounds throughout the year, it gets hot starting in late summer when the adult salmon start their run. Then in December the steelhead come into the river from the sea. Clusters of salmon roe, spinners, and spoons work well for both fish. A fine Game Department access point for bank fishing can be reached off state Rte. 109, where you turn on the road paralleling the railroad tracks on the east side and drive to COPALIS CROSSING. You can launch your boat for leisurely float trips (which the natives contend is the best way to fish the river) at two other excellent access spots: One point is eight miles northeast of the town of Humptulips where Donkey Creek Road crosses the river's west fork; another is at the railroad bridge just south of the town. You can float a few miles farther downstream to the Gouchners access point on the west side of the river. These are beautiful trips through unspoiled terrain.

The other river right here that we like is the WISHKAH, which has several points of access from the road heading north alongside it out of ABERDEEN. About six miles up is a good access point. The fishing picks up in late summer for salmon and in early winter for steelhead. Pulp mill pollution near Cosmopolis has severely hurt the fishing on the Chehalis, Satsop, and Wynoochee rivers.

INTO INDIAN COUNTRY

About forty miles north are the QUINAULT RIVER and LAKE QUINAULT. At the lodge on the lake you can arrange for Indian guides on the lower river. There has been some recent logging along the river that has damaged its waters, but the new Logging Practices Act promises to cure that problem. Above the lake, salmon, steelhead, and Dolly Varden bite well on flies and spoons. The lake has its moments, but they aren't that often. Instead, we'd recommend you drive another twenty-five miles to the QUEETS RIVER. Glaciers high in the Olympic National Park feed the Queets and give it an even flow throughout the year. The fishing, too, is good year-round. You can get any of the different fish native to the peninsula here, and the road off U.S.101 that parallels the river offers many ready access points. The Queets is good for fly fishing, spin casting, or bait fishing; and because most of it is in the national forest no license is required — only the state's salmon and steelhead punch cards. A beautiful hike can be made from road's end upstream, and the fishing improves the farther you go.

The HOH RIVER parallels the road leading off Rte. 101 to the OLYMPIC NATIONAL PARK headquarters. It's a sensational drive — possibly the state's most beautiful stretch — and there are many riffles and pools to stop and fish. Or there are incredibly scenic hikes upstream from the headquarters. This is a rain forest, and annual precipitation exceeds a hundred inches. The Hoh is one of the top rivers in the state and you can catch everything from jack salmon that scale around three pounds in the summer to huge king salmon to forty pounds in the fall, from prized steelhead and cutthroat trout to Dolly Varden. We already discussed the drive along the Hoh west of Rte. 101 in our introduction to the state, and we'll only add here that at the mouth of the river you can watch the Indians working their fishing nets.

On north, the BOGACHIEL and SOLEDUCK RIVERS often

provide as exciting a fishery as the Hoh. In the town of FORKS, you can hire guides for both rivers, but we recommend that effort only during the height of steelhead season in December and January. You can find some good bank fishing along Bogachiel Road that leads to the Bogachiel rearing pond or by parking at the Bogachiel State Park on 101. A boat is needed to do the Soleduck justice, but one good bank fishing stretch can be readily reached by turning east off Rte. 101 two miles north of Forks and then bearing to your left at the junction a mile and a half up.

West of PORT ANGELES two spots produce good fishing, LAKE SUTHERLAND for lunker cutthroat and the ELWHA RIVER for steelhead and salmon. Sutherland has a fine resort and boat facilities. During the spring and fall go after the big cutthroats with spinners, worms, or plugs. During nearly the entire year, the Elwha yields fine cutthroat trout and jack salmon; but it, like the other peninsula streams, is best during the salmon and steelhead runs. You can get to its east bank by heading west out of Port Angeles on Rte. 112 for a couple of miles and then turning right at the bridge.

THE PUGET SOUND

The huge bay or sound is one of those spectacular places of nature. Its great fir and hemlock trees and sparkling waters reflect snow-capped mountains — postcard scenes of the highest order. Streams pour billions of gallons of fresh water into the sound daily in exchange for exciting runs of bright salmon and game steelhead making their way from the open sea to their spawning grounds high in the Olympic and Cascade mountains. During past years the Puget Sound's fishery has suffered from pulp mill pollution and the loss of marshy estuaries, which became landfills for housing developments. Progress is not to be blamed, but rather man's inability to control progress. Most knowledgeable people now agree that the decimation of plankton and crustaceans has probably bottomed out and the food chain is being revitalized. Still, the fishing has always remained good and fast, and state biologists figure it is now improving dramatically.

Selecting the best rivers and lakes in this area is misleading because most of them often get hot. Generally, the most popular rivers yield the most fish — that is, the rivers that statistically provide the most fish are indeed fished most often. Perennially the Green and Skagit are at the top of the list for steelhead, but the Puyallup, Stillaguamish, and Skykomish boast tremendous fish too. A standout for trout, Ross Lake heads the Skagit River, sprawling north about twenty miles to the Canadian border. It is remote and has had comparatively light fishing pressure, which means it has big trout. In the northwest corner of the state, Whatcom and Big Lakes also produce bragging-size bass. The state record 10½-pound bass was lifted from Whatcom Lake.

Counterclockwise: Chinook, Steelhead and Coho Jacks.
WASHINGTON DEPARTMENT OF FISHERIES

Going after steelhead is a painstaking process, and the diehards here report that they have often spent an entire season without hooking into a good one. But it's the experience of landing a fifteen- or twenty-pounder that hooks these anglers. My exposure was on a day when a fresh snow covered the ground, tipping the branches of the evergreens. With the crisp, February morning air it seemed a day more fitting for hunting than fishing — but then, I wasn't yet a Washington steelhead stalwart.

SEARCHING OUT STEELHEADS

We launched our fourteen-foot boat on the Skagit River near CONCRETE, a town that no longer has too much life, because the plant for which it was named no longer operates. The people there, however, haven't had great cause for concern, since this country is only a couple of hours from Seattle (north on Rte. I-5 and then east on 20), and an hour from some parts of the metropolitan area. We were using salmon eggs, fishing the riffles and the smooth glides, moving frequently, but not so often we didn't give the sea-run rainbow a chance to hit if they were in the hole. I was finding out what the native knows: Steelheading is not like salmon fishing. The steelhead are wily and, even if you hook one, hardly easy to land.

Toward the middle of the afternoon I was lazing back against the boat's gunwale, sunning my face when my pole was nearly ripped from my hand. Line was whirring out and I caught a blister on my thumb — I didn't know about that until later, however. It was a fight. Steelhead are not jumpers, but they swim deep and hard and, like any great trout, look for ways to snag up your line. For long minutes I worked to stop this one's run. Just when I thought I had him in hand, finally, he darted for a log. My line was snagged, and in seconds the fish was gone. Strangely, I didn't feel too badly about it; after all, I'd known the thrill of the stout steelhead, felt his immense strength and quick speed. And that explosive power and instinctive wile. I knew enough to be a steelheader. A good steelhead is a sportsman's challenge, a true fighting fish of the first rank.

STARTING FROM SEATTLE

We figure most people heading into the Puget Sound area will hit Seattle first, so we'll take you through some fine waters right near the metropolitan core and then north into the great steelhead rivers. After we hit the Canadian border, we'll again drop to Seattle and take you south along the sound and then cross its lower reaches and move back north on the western side.

In and around Seattle the big fish is the salmon, and lately the best fishing has been for sockeye salmon in LAKE WASHINGTON, just west of Bellevue. This huge lake (once sorely polluted but now a showcase of sparkling waters that prove man can take care of himself) produces all kinds of freshwater and sea-run fish, but five-pound sockeyes are the best bet. Bass prefer the shallows of Juanita and Yarrow bays along the eastern shore. Farther offshore on the eastern side and up to the mouth of the Sammamish River at the north end, lightning-fast Kokanee salmon (landlocked sockeye) especially like small periwinkles on tiny hooks. You can launch a boat at several parks and Game Department access points, notably on the Sammamish River near Bothell and the Cedar River at RENTON. Just to the east of Lake Washington is LAKE SAMMAMISH, which is best known for its silver trout, as they call the Kokanee. Boat rentals are available along Rte. 901, and the best fishing spots are at either the north or south ends of the lake. Or you can head north from Sammamish State Park near ISSAQUAH for a few miles and reach Pine Lake, which is well stocked with catchable rainbow trout. Wilderness Lake is thirty miles south on Rte. 169 near MAPLE VALLEY, and it's excellent for seeking rainbows from its banks.

Much of the sport in this area comes from the wide variety of fishing. Between AUBURN and Summit off Rte. 169 is Lake Sawyer, a year-round hot spot for perch. If you like fishing rivers and streams, which the local fishermen like better than their lakes, catchable rainbow are stocked in the CEDAR RIVER southeast of Maple Valley. These rivers are good for flies, bait, or spinning lures. In December, January, and

February, the SNOQUALMIE RIVER — thirty minutes north on Rte. 203 — has a good steelhead run. The fish hatchery road between FALL CITY and Snoqualmie puts you into a good bank fishing spot; another good access to the Snoqualmie is in the King County Park at Carnation. Salmon eggs, spoons, flies, and fluorescent spin-glo lures can work. Try to bump your lure along the river's bottom; or if other folks are using heavy weights, give it a shot by merely increasing the weight of your drop sinker. The Snoqualmie River, however, is overshadowed in this locale by the GREEN RIVER, traditionally one of the state's top three steelhead rivers. One popular spot on the Green is west of PALMER, and a couple of other fine accesses lie along the road that turns west off Rte. 169 south of BLACK DIAMOND just before you reach the river. Where you see other cars pulled off the road, it's a sure sign someone knows of a good hole. In previous years, the Green has been primarily a winter-run steelhead river, but the summer run has been picking up and six- to fifteen-pounders are expected in good numbers. Steelhead fishing is an art of its own, and in steelheading the best fishermen are the ones with yards of patience.

THE GREAT STEELHEAD RIVERS

Driving north from the Seattle area, turn right off Rte. 522 toward MONROE. After five miles on Rte. 202 you will hit "the forks" of the SKYKOMISH RIVER at the Cathcart Snoqualmie Road, where there are fine runs of both summer and winter steelhead. Salmon and Dolly Varden also hit in the fall months. The stretch of the river east of Monroe to INDEX off Rte. 2 is accessible at a boat-launching ramp at Sultan. There is good access from the road northeast of Index that parallels the north fork, which has good rainbow and steelhead fishing from June to September. A bronze wobbler spoon is a favorite here.

Moving north on Rte. I-5, Silver and Martha Lakes lie five miles south of EVERETT. They have good trout and Kokanee; and both boat and resort accommodations are available. Just to the east, winter steelhead can be caught on the Snohomish River near the town of Snohomish.

Five miles north of MARYSVILLE turn west to Goodwin Lake where you have a chance at huge, trophy rainbows weighing as much as ten pounds. Boats can be rented at the state park, and the fishing is best in spring and fall. A bit more to the north at SILVANA, where Pilchuk Creek flows into the STILL-AGUAMISH RIVER, old-timers like to use salmon eggs for summer and winter steelhead. Take Norman Road east off Rte. 530 to the river. The anglers here use spinners, worms, and salmon eggs — and usually some huge whoppers are landed. If you have a fly rod, head northeast out of ARLINGTON on Rte. 530 to test the north fork of the Stillaguamish, especially for summer steelhead and sea-run cutthroat. Numerous blind roads branch off the main road, and they'll put you at the river where chest-waders are great to have along. Or if you went southeast out of ARLINGTON on either Stehr or Jordan road, you could fish for winter "steelies" on either fork of the river. Farther upstream, fifteen miles east of Granite Falls, you reach SIL-VERTON in the Glacier Peak Wilderness. The forest service campgrounds are plentiful and there are nice hikes into Helena and North lakes in the mountains. In late July and August the cutthroat trout bite well. A rubber raft and spinning gear would be the ideal equipment for these lakes. Back toward Arlington and near the Navy communications station, Twin Lakes offers cutthroat fishing. At the town of TRAFTON, take the Trafton Road southeast.

THE SUPERB SKAGIT RIVER

The best steelhead river, the grand SKAGIT, pours into the Sound five miles west of Rte. I-5 at CONWAY. Every year thousands of steelhead are caught on this spectacular river, and the salmon and sea-run cutthroat trout fishing is also good. This river has all types of northwoods angling: high-mountain torrents rushing into the main stream, dammed up tributaries that form beautiful lakes surrounded by lush evergreens, the meandering yet rushing main river in the coastal flatlands. The winter run of steelhead is dynamite from December to April, and then a couple of months later the summer run heads up river. Salmon and cutthroat trout take up any slack in the spring and summer months. At the mouth, the resort called Phil's Boathouse down Fir Island Road offers camping, boat rentals, and supplies. Here you can hook steelhead up to twenty-five pounds and king salmon up to fifty. If you aren't an experienced steelhead fisherman, you might still catch one off Young's Bar north on Baker Street in the town of MOUNT VERNON. Use a couple of ounces of lead and drop a leader off a foot above the sinker; your bait could be salmon eggs attached to a hook with yarn or a floating artificial lure. One youngster at the bar with a five-dollar rod and reel, cast a split shot and earthworm out about ten feet and pulled in a twelve-pound steelie.

It nearly always takes patience to nail big salmon and steelhead; and we'd recommend that you try several spots along the river: SEDRO WOOLEY, CONCRETE, VAN HORN, and SAUK, though the natives catch them all along the banks. Boats are popular, and public access for launching is available at nearly all towns. There's good lake fishing here too. BIG LAKE off Rte. 9 sports big bass, trout, and perch. Grassy shorelines and cattails provide a haven for bass up to six pounds. North a few miles is Clear Lake where rainbow trout and bass are plentiful.

Heading west from Mount Vernon on Rte. 536, several lakes offer quality fishing. In the Spring and fall Campbell and Pass Lakes near ANACORTES are especially good. Campbell holds perch and bass, and it's a delightful, beautiful setting where you can get a cabin and a boat. Pass Lake in the Deception Pass State Park has long been a favorite of fly fishermen. At DECEPTION PASS — where the tidal waters rush in and out — saltwater varieties of bass and cod can be caught on jigs and pork rind cast from the shore. And from the beach between GREENBANK and FREELAND, you'll find one of the few places you can cast for steelhead in salt water. A good drive past MARBLEMOUNT northeast on Rte. 20 gets you to Mineral Park and Marble Creek campgrounds on the banks of the CASCADE RIVER. These are ideal spots for family fishing and camping, and the trout fishing turns fast in August and September.

The giant ROSS LAKE lies farther north on Rte. 20. This lake has never been heavily fished, and it holds large rainbow trout weighing as much as five pounds. The fishing is best near the mouths of the tributary streams. Access is being improved to the lake from the highway, but for years you could only get to it on logging roads cut down from Canada or by ferry boat from Diablo Dam. Be sure to check the specific angling regulations. Below Ross, Diablo Lake can be good for rainbows in the spring. Another good lake, not quite so removed, is just north of Concrete. Baker Lake rainbows like both flies and lures, and hit best in early summer.

LARGEMOUTHS IN LAKE WHATCOM

Farther north up Rte. I-5 lies famous Lake Whatcom on the east edge of BELLINGHAM. Largemouth bass to 10½ pounds have been pulled from its depths, particularly in its swampy north corner. Cutthroat trout to six pounds forage along the steep drop-offs in the south part of the lake. You can arrange boat rentals and lodging at Bellingham. Nearby Lake Samish is frequently hot for bass, Kokanee, and trout. If you want catfish for dinner, drive north from Bellingham and then west to Lake Terrell. In late summer and fall, hikers can enjoy the scenic splendor of the high Cascades and high-quality cutthroat trout fishing on the Chain Lakes near MOUNT BAKER, a 10,778-foot dormant volcano. The slopes of Mount Baker are remote, and the lake fishing is good. Driving east on Rte. 542, turn north at MAPLE FALLS to reach Silver Lake, which has a fine park on its west bank. You should be able to get a limit of trout in the fall. Farther east to SHUKSAN, a steep mountain road climbs to Twin Lakes, another fine trout lake. Check your brakes before making this thrilling trip. Late summer is about right, and any other time the lake could be frozen tight. But then, who are we to discourage ice fishing?

SOUTH FROM SEATTLE

Now back to Seattle to cover the southern half of Puget Sound and its western shoreline. First, we should mention that salmon fishing in the sound can be good. But it's a huge body of water, and we'd recommend a guide of some sort if you expect to catch many fish.

East of TACOMA, some winter steelheading spots on the PUYALLUP RIVER are off the North Levee Road at many places. Look for cars pulled off the road and join the action.

THE EASTERN OLYMPIC PENINSULA

Rte. 101 out of Olympia winds northwest into the more remote Olympic Peninsula. The adventurous can find hundreds of miles of trails and roads into the Olympic National Forest, and the fishing at these high-country spots can be superb. August and April are good months to fish the mouth of the SKOKOMISH RIVER near Union. Cutthroats from seven to fifteen inches give a lot of action on light spinning gear during the late summer; the steelhead enter the river for their summer run in April. You will need to get a fee permit because this is an Indian reservation. Also during late April and through May, drive another ten miles to the northwest to LAKE CUSHMAN where the cutthroats are dynamite. A resort and park are there north of Hoodsport. Price Lake is only a short drive from here, and in October some excellent rainbow and brook trout can be hooked on flies.

Several lakes lie to the east near BELFAIR on Rte. 3. On opening day, which is usually the third Sunday in April, hundreds of fishermen line the banks and jam boats to pull out thousands of trout — those catchable eight- to twelve-inch trout. Mission Lake is regarded as one of the hotter spots, and Bay Lake (where boats are available) north of Longbranch is another. Farther north up Rte. 101, you'll find the QUILCENE RIVER near the town of Quilcene. There are several easy hikes off the highway and access is good. From July through January good catches of cutthroat, salmon, and steelhead are made. Tarboo Lake, east of QUILCENE off Rte. 104, is another fine opening day trout lake. All of these trout lakes are good as the state periodically stocks them.

SOUTHWESTERN WASHINGTON

Just south of towering Mount Rainier lies Washington's back country, rural hamlets where legends and weird happenings continuously sprout and grow. It is so rugged, well . . .

The now infamous D.B. Cooper, the skyjacker who bailed out with $200,000 never to be seen again, either escaped easily or met death here. The natives of such towns as Battleground, Green Mountain, and Brush Prairie say that this dense, rugged mountain country is so impenetrable, his fate may never be known. Here, too, the natives believe in "Big foot," or Sasquatch as they call him.

Sasquatch is a half-ape, half-man creature who leaves twenty-inch footprints, raids camps, and has even been photographed on rare occasions. Legions of Sasquatch hunters often hit the back hills looking for his tracks, and they've reported seeing him on scores of occasions. Again the folks here know the country is so deep that it could hide a Sasquatch family from prying eyes indefinitely. They used to laugh at themselves here when they said they believed in Sasquatch. Today they don't.

The fishing is as wild as the country. Swift Creek Reservoir is a beautiful lake nestled in the midst of towering pine and fir. Some fishermen here claim no one has left Swift Creek without the limit of rainbow in years, which may be stretching the truth but not all that much. Here runs the Cowlitz River, too, the state's top stream. Depending on the time of year, you can catch most any kind of fish you want — from steelhead to salmon, cutthroat to rainbow trout. The variety of this southwestern corner is astounding: The mighty Columbia offers terrific fishing from sandbars, steelhead rivers seem countless. Drano Lake near Cook is the only place where fishermen troll successfully for steelhead, and the Gifford-Pinchot National Forest around Mount Adams gives stout hikers the chance to get away from everything, except perhaps Sasquatch.

SALMON CAPITOL OF THE WORLD

But even farther west, at the mouth of the COLUMBIA RIVER, lies the "salmon fishing capitol of the world." If ever a fisherman could come close to having a guaranteed catch, it

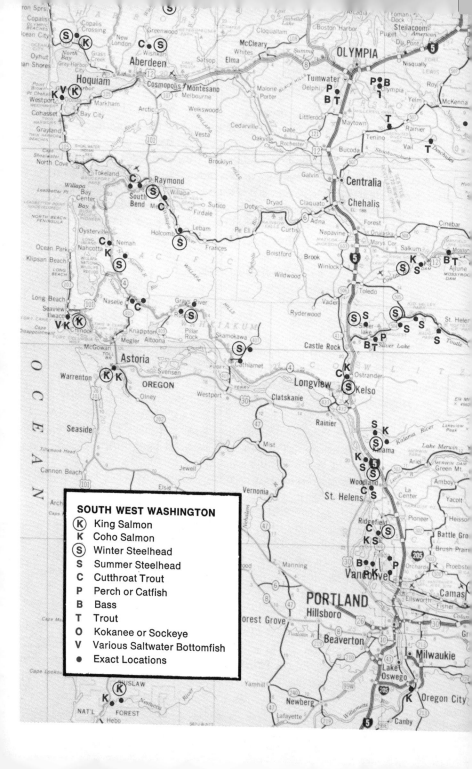

SOUTH WEST WASHINGTON

- Ⓚ King Salmon
- K Coho Salmon
- Ⓢ Winter Steelhead
- S Summer Steelhead
- C Cutthroat Trout
- P Perch or Catfish
- B Bass
- T Trout
- O Kokanee or Sockeye
- V Various Saltwater Bottomfish
- • Exact Locations

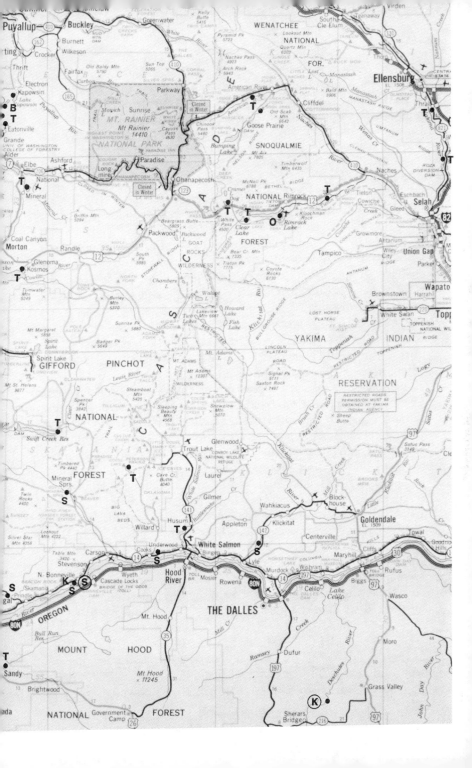

would be from the party boats that put out daily from ILWACO and WESTPORT during the salmon season. Starting in mid-April, the mighty king salmon start appearing off the Columbia, and they'll often go sixty or seventy pounds. By late July the more plentiful but smaller — ten- to twenty-pound — coho or silver salmon check in. Generally any time during summer and early fall the boats head out at 6 A.M. and return with most fishermen sporting their limit of three.

There's a lot of inland streams between Ilwaco and Westport, but the best rivers are the NASELLE, NORTH NEMAH, and WILLAPA. The Naselle has some of the best sea-run cutthroat trout, and from July to November it's common to catch a stringer of eighteen- to twenty-inchers. The bigger trout are caught here trolling or casting spinners and worms in tidal waters. There's a boat launch at NASELLE, and you can get to the bank at spots all along the road leading upstream from town. A better stream for fall and winter fishing lies just to the north, the NORTH NEMAH RIVER. A boat can be launched where Rte. 101 crosses the river, or you can follow the road east along the river. It's good wading, but stay below the Finn Creek Hatchery. Good bait may be a bronze wobbler, fresh salmon eggs, or other drift-fishing rigs. Be sure to check state fishing regulations since many of these rivers have varying seasons, and portions of the streams may be restricted. Father north at RAYMOND, you'll hit the WILLAPA, which produces jack salmon and cutthroats from late summer to winter and steelhead during the winter. Boat launches are at Raymond, Wilson Creek Landing, and the Narrows. The best fishing comes an hour either side of low tide. Follow Rte. 6 east to LEBAM and you'll see some access points in easy walking distance, particularly two or three miles downstream of town. Steelhead up to twenty pounds in the winter will often go for salmon-egg clusters in early morning and on cloudy days, particularly if you let them drift with the current.

THE COLUMBIA RIVER TRIBUTARIES

If you drive east on Rte. 4 along the broad Columbia, you will find many fine rivers. The rivers here just keep coming — and so do the fish. Unlike California and Nevada, where so many fishermen crowd the streams and lakes for eight- to ten-inch trout, these rivers provide a true test. The native fish are wily, especially the salmon and steelhead — mature, wise, and full of fight. The pristine settings of meandering streams amidst tall evergreens make the experience all the more memorable. All of these rivers hold sea-run cutthroat, salmon, and winter and summer steelhead, but you need to check fishing regulations to learn when and where certain rivers are closed.

Closest to the coastline, the GRAYS RIVER has a good run of winter steelhead — that seagoing cousin of the rainbow trout. At Grays River turn south to Kessler Road, cross the bridge, and you will find a public fishing hole. Or take Rte. 830 east from Grays River and, after crossing a bridge, take the first left on Maks Road. About one mile further, there's another fishing hole. At CATHLAMET, two good winter steelheading access points on the Elochoman River can be found driving north on Rte. 407.

Willapa Bay Chinook ranging from 28-40 pounds.
WASHINGTON DEPARTMENT OF FISHERIES

The COWLITZ RIVER, the lower Columbia's biggest tributary, runs swiftly in its upper reaches but turns slow and deep in the lower waters near Ostrander and Kelso. Fishing is best on cloudy days and the river is superb for either the fisherman in a boat or on the bank. More fish — of all kinds — are caught here than any other place in the state. There's a county park off the east side of Rte. 411 north of LONGVIEW; or drive north toward CASTLE ROCK, stopping wherever you see a number of cars pulled off the road — a sure sign something unusual is happening; and it's usually that the fish are hitting. A few miles east of Rte. I-5 on Rte. 504 at SILVER LAKE, stop at Anderson's for guided Cowlitz boat fishing trips in a jet sled or rent a boat to go after trout, catfish, and bass — they like to feed in and around patches of lily pads. The most dependable fishing may be in June and September at the salmon hatchery near SALKUM on Rte 12, east of the interstate. You can fish from either bank, but you need a boat to reach the southeast shore.

The TOUTLE RIVER, a tributary of the Cowlitz, has superb bank fishing year-round: the campground at the forks at Coal Bank Bridge, for example, or farther upstream at ST. HELENS. Flies work well in May and June. At the KALAMA RIVER, boat launches and bank fishing are at the Modrow Bridge, Hatchery Creek, and where the Spencer Creek Road hits the river. To change the pace, you'll find fine sandbar fishing on the Columbia River at Kalama, WOODLAND, and Frenchman's Bar north of Vancouver. Too, Vancouver Lake is especially good in the spring for catfish, which often lurk along the south shore.

THE GORGEOUS COLUMBIA GORGE

At Vancouver, the Columbia begins its transformation from a broad, lazy river to a faster-running torrent. Before the numerous dams slowed it down, the river carved a beautiful gorge between Oregon and Washington. Driving through this country is breathtaking, and vantage points make excellent picnicking spots. Often a small state or county park will nestle along a road with a sparkling waterfall only a few yards away. This is one place where you should get off the interstate highway on the Oregon side.

As you drive east from Vancouver on Rte. 14, you will first come to the Washougal River, which is historically a fine producer of summer steelhead. On Rte. 140, two miles north of the town of Washougal, or where 140 crosses the river at Canyon Creek near Prindle, try wading and using a floating fly line during the summer. Further east on Rte. 14 brings you to the first of the Columbia's dams, the Bonneville. In early June use jigs and spoons for steelhead and trout just below the dam.

At Carson, the Wind River rushes to meet the Columbia. It holds fine steelheads in July and August. Since both the Washougal and Wind rivers have roads paralleling them, watch for concentrations of cars — it nearly always indicates the steelhead fishermen have found a hot hole. A mile east of Cooks, you can put your boat into Drano Lake, where trolling during the summer often hooks big steelhead. Stay on Rte. 14 for another 20 miles east and you will reach Lyle and the Klickitat River. The Klickitat has summer steelhead often weighing up to twelve pounds; but occasionally the river gets mucked up with silt so check first with the regional Game Department agent by phone.

THE WILD BACKCOUNTRY

Some of the best lake fishing in the state is found in the densely forested hills and mountains between the Columbia and towering Mt. Rainier. This is the home of Sasquatch, or Bigfoot, that fast-roaming creature sighted hundreds of times throughout the Northwest. Instead of following Rte. 14 east from the Vancouver-Portland area, drive north on I-5 to where Rte. 503 heads east.

The road skirts the northern edge of first Lake Merwin and then Yale Lake, often climbing hundreds of feet above the lakes and the view, well, it has to be seen. We recommend that you bypass Merwin and Yale and drive another few miles to Swift Creek Reservoir, which reputedly guarantees limits of trout. A good boat-launching site is at the east end of the road out of Cougar.

LAKE FISHING FOR TROUT

To the north along Rte. 12 east of I-5, two large lakes, MAY-FIELD and DAVISSON, have both trout and bass. In the early morning, if you quietly and stealthily sneak up on the upper end of Mayfield, you often can see nice-sized bass swimming in the shallows. There are rough boat launches on both lakes. About thirty miles farther north, you'll find two more lakes, McIntosh to the west and Lawrence to the east of the town of RAINIER. These two are among the better early summer fishing lakes for trout, and both have good public access for both bank and boat angling.

Early season fly fishing can turn red hot on several lakes south of KAPOWSIN, about thirty miles southeast of Tacoma. Take the Eatonville-Kapowsin Road to Kapowsin, Tanwax, Clear, and Ohop lakes. During the warm summer months these lakes also offer bass fishing. West of EATONVILLE drive to MCKENNA on Rte. 702 and take the Harts Lake Loop Road to get into early summer bass fishing in Silver and Harts lakes. Both lakes have boats, camping, and lodging facilities. South on Rte. I-5, you might take the Lacy exit, following Patterson Way to Patterson and Long Lakes. They are good for casting or bait fishing for bass, catfish, and trout. Again, all kinds of facilities and accommodations are available. Moving west, the Black River, just beyond OLYMPIA, is productive for black bass, trout, and catfish.

FOR THE PURIST

For the fisherman who likes to hike back into nature, the prettiest and most remote part of this southwestern section of the state is in the GIFFORD PINCHOT NATIONAL FOREST. If you follow the Columbia gorge east to White Salmon, turn north on Rte. 141 to TROUT LAKE, where you jump off on forest roads. This is high-country lake fishing where spinners, cheese bait, and flies work superbly. First, get a map at the ranger station and look for South Prairie, Forlorn, and GOOSE Lakes in the south part of the forest: Mosquito Lake in the central portion; and Council, Takhlakh, Olallie, Chain of Lakes, and Horseshoe to the north. The trails are good and so is the huckleberry picking in late August. After Labor Day, the weather turns. And before July, you'll find heavy frost when you wake after a night under the stars.

THE CASCADE EASTERN SLOPE

The eastern slope of the Cascade Mountrains, much of it lush national forest land, is perfect for one of those great retreats into rugged high country. You won't find the sport of hooking big steelhead and salmon on this side of the mountains, but you will find those fast-running, white-water streams where trout thrive. We'll discuss several streams here, but paramount is the Methow River, a rollicking river that tumbles and twists down the slopes of 8,760-foot Gardner Mountain. Its headwaters form near Rainy Pass in the Okanogan National Forest, and for twenty-five miles from Mazama it parallels Rte. 20. From the July Fourth weekend through the early fall it is one of the state's most popular family fishing and camping sites. It's best to fish the pools and riffles with flies, spinners, and bait. What you will catch are those pan-size rainbow trout, one after another.

The rainbow is a glamorous fish to catch, and the fishing is especially fine because of the state's stocking programs. Though these trout are hatchery-raised and planted in catchable sizes, they are indeed trout. They can see a careless fisherman on the bank, they can hear too much racket, and they can be wily. One of the reasons worms and salmon eggs make such fine bait is the trout's liking for anything red or pink in color. The California Department of Fish and Game Biologists have even proven that trout can see and are attracted by red objects entirely out of the water. Trout have a fine sense of smell — one reason why live bait is often the best — and they do taste their food. The fish will take anything that looks like food to them into their mouths, but they will only swallow what tastes good. Fortunately, the trout isn't a fast thinker, particularly when it comes to touch sensations. This accounts for the fish often hitting the same hook repeatedly, and it leads some biologists to contend that trout do not experience pain sensations as we know them.

This eastern slope abounds with good spots to pursue trout. The Twisp, Chiwawa, and Wenatchee rivers compare with the Methow, and you will certainly find plenty of beautiful places to wade in for fishing. This is pretty country so any of these rivers and lakes make for a grand outing. The lakes, Conconully and Spectacle, are especially good in spring and fall. In December the resort at Roses Lake by Chelan attracts knowledgeable local anglers. Whitestone Lake north of Tonasket is the only good bass lake in the region and its shallow areas are superb for surface plugs.

THE GRAND COULEE AREA

About thirty-five miles southwest of famed Grand Coulee Dam lies JAMESON LAKE, a fine fishing lake good for action as early as April and May, and then again in September and October. The rainbow here run as large as five pounds — a huge fighting fish. Both bank and boat fishermen have good luck with flies and nightcrawlers. Resorts are at both ends of the lake, and there is a public launching area for boats at the south end.

Head west from Jameson, through WENATCHEE to CASH-MERE on the west side of the Columbia, and you quickly reach a fine trout river, the WENATCHEE. The fishing action heats up about the Fourth of July, and it's excellent into the fall. Some nice summer steelhead also run the Wenatchee in the fall, and you can suddenly find yourself in one of those challenges where you've a whopper on light trout gear and only skill will bring him home.

We like to think that a fisherman needs to spend nearly as much time preparing for his expedition as he does in his boat or wading hip-deep in the rushing white water. What is the sense, after all, of ending up on a small, babbling brook loaded with eight- to fourteen-inch rainbow trout with only a rod and reel capable of horsing in a twenty-five-pound salmon. Fishing is a sport, and only when the fisherman establishes himself as a sportsman can he truly enjoy the thrill and exhilaration of fishing. One Washington old-timer told me that the greatest afternoon he ever spent was on the Wenatchee River: He had taken out light fly fishing gear all set for the small rainbows that can create so much havoc with the fly and tender line. For an hour he had delighted in the sport of catching three pan-size rainbows. He had known that his two-pound test line wouldn't stand too much horsing of these trout, particularly if one dipped beneath a log or into some undergrowth. Then suddenly, he knew he had a different challenge on his hands. The wet fly he was using had disappeared and his line had started snaking off his reel. He could feel the strength of his fish, and he knew it must be a big one. There was a look of pure delight on his face as he told of spending the better part of an hour bringing in a 7½-pound steelhead. "Hell, I've caught twenty-pounders before, but I've never caught anything like a seven-pounder on two-pound test. I decided early on that he wouldn't break my line and that if he was going to get away, it was going to be because I hadn't hooked him well to start with." That's the kind of fishing challenge we all hope for. And that's the reason why we feel you should spend a few minutes thinking ahead of time about the gear you need to catch the fish you're after. It can make the difference.

UP THE WENATCHEE

Up the Wenatchee are some fine family camping grounds, particularly in the Wenatchee National Forest, and the catchable trout make it great for the youngsters. The CHIWAWA RIVER feeds the Wenatchee just above the town of PLAIN on Rte. 209. It's good fishing upstream to GROUSE CREEK CAMP. This river, like the Wenatchee, opens the Fourth of July. Just west of the Chiwawa is Fish Lake, which is renowned as one of the finest lakes in the state for the delicious perch. To the northeast, two lakes near the towns of CHELAN and MANSON on Rte. 150 have fine resorts and public access. Wapato Lake is good summer trout fishing, and Roses Lake is known locally for its winter trout fishing — a good combination.

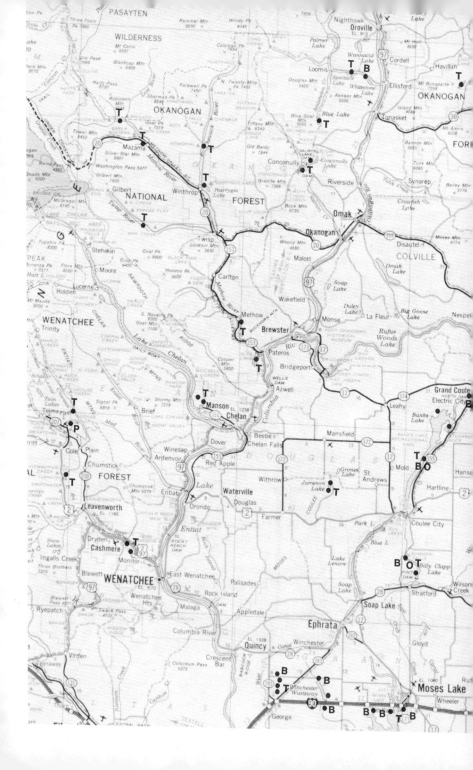

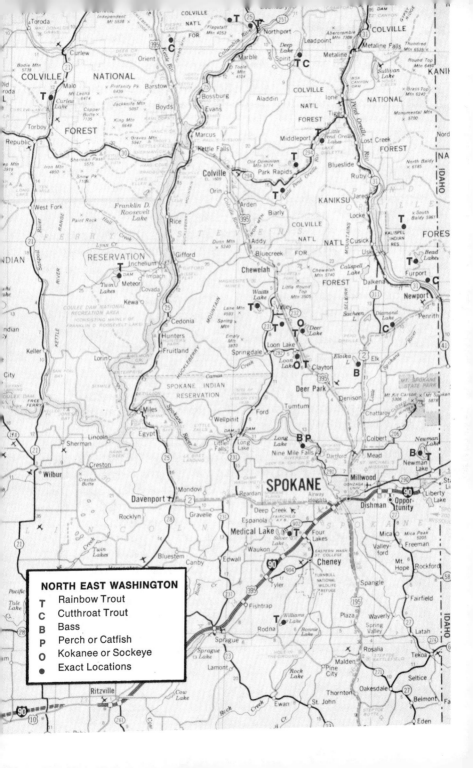

NORTH EAST WASHINGTON

T	Rainbow Trout
C	Cutthroat Trout
B	Bass
P	Perch or Catfish
O	Kokanee or Sockeye
●	Exact Locations

At PATEROS — seventeen miles to the north of Chelan on Rte. 97 and the next door to where the METHOW RIVER flows into the Columbia — nestles ALTA LAKE, superb for spring trout fishing. It has fine resorts, camping, and boat-launching access. But if you get this close to the METHOW RIVER, you simply can't give it the cold shoulder. Because of its terrific fishing for rainbow, it's a must from Independence Day into October. Both Rtes. 153 and 20 in the Okanogan National Forest provide ready access. A forest service road jumps off at MAZAMA on Rte. 20 and parallels the beautiful fast-flowing gravel-bottom stream for miles, with excellent access all along to RIVER BEND campground. The TWISP RIVER, just to the southwest of the Methow, is also a fine rainbow stream and it also has good camping and bank fishing access.

The lake fishing here just may be as good as most of the river angling. All of these lakes are full of rainbow trout. By WINTHROP, on Rte. 20, PEARRYGIN LAKE has a couple of resorts, a state park, and some fine fishing. If you head east to OKANOGAN and cut west halfway to OMAK, you'll be on the route to CONCONULLY LAKE and Conconully Reservoir, where all facilities are available. Farther north of Conconully lie Fish and BLUE Lakes.

You have to head nearly to the Canadian border here to find anything but rainbow. SPECTACLE and WHITESTONE lakes sparkle amidst stands of pine and fir, lying between LOOMIS and ELLISFORD on Rte. 97. Spectacle has some really fine lunker rainbows that you'll have a time landing and you'll have an equally good time showing off. Whitestone sports good bass and crappie with the shallow west end just right for surface lures. To the east, in the shadow of 7,258-foot BONAPARTE MOUNTAIN lies BONAPARTE LAKE. Take the road to the north off Rte. 30 that parallels Bonaparte Creek. Bonaparte provides variety — eastern brook trout, mackinaw as they call their lake trout, and Kokanee. There's a boat launch and resort there. East on Rte. 30 turn north on Rte. 21 to CURLEW LAKE for good trout fishing during summer months.

THE COLUMBIA FLATS

For most of its first two hundred and fifty miles the majestic Columbia River carves a deep, ruggedly spectacular gorge between Oregon and Washington. The Columbia then swings north into Washington's broad eastern valley, where it has been dammed and tapped for irrigation waters. Strangely, some of the water started disappearing, though not so many people noticed it until suddenly it started surfacing at the most unaccountable places. This seepage area today — this valley bottom land with hundreds of swampy ponds and lakes — has become one of the top bass fishing places in the country.

They call all of this between the towns of Moses Lake and Royal City "The Potholes," and it's a superb setting for fish and waterfowl. The Columbia National Wildlife Refuge is here. For an area of fifty square miles the water has literally taken over, and it is a marvelous phenomenon for the fisherman. Bass hit year-round on plugs, plastic worms, and surface lures, and the fishing is equally good from boat or bank.

Kokanee and trout fishing sparkle here too. At Cle Elum, Kachess, and Keechelus Lakes you have a bonus limit of twenty Kokanee. The reason is that Kokanee reproduce so marvelously that fishing pressure is seldom great enough to keep the numbers of fish down. The more Kokanee or landlocked sockeye salmon in a lake, the smaller they grow. And at Cle Elum you can troll for lake trout that grow as large as twenty pounds. And as in most parts of Washington, there are national forests with quick streams that make for splendid day-long hikes. The rainbow in these charming brooks are plentiful and so easy to catch you often only need marshmallows and a willow switch. The best of these trout streams are in Snoqualmie National Forest and the Crab Creek Wildlife Recreation Area.

THE COLUMBIA AT THE TRI-CITIES
The Columbia is joined by the Snake River at the tri-cities' area of RICHLAND, PASCO, and KENNEWICK. We'll talk

about the Snake in our next section, but the COLUMBIA upriver from PASCO at RINGOLD, holds good salmon and summer steelhead, and the fishing for them is best from September through November. You will have to start on the map of southeastern Washington, and as you drive north shift to the northeastern map. Another fifty miles upstream, northwest, there's good fall bank fishing for steelhead just south of Wanapum Dam to the mouth of Crab Creek. About two miles to the east lie three little-known lakes — Lenice, Mary, and Nunally in the CRAB CREEK WILDLIFE RECREATION AREA. They require just the proper sporting hike — in fact, many people portage canoes in on their shoulders — and from April to July 15 and then again in October and November, these lakes turn hot for exceptionally nice rainbows. The trout run up to twenty-four inches in length; and the limit is three, all more than twelve inches long.

THE BEST BASS FISHING

It's a forty-mile drive east on Rte. 26 to OTHELLO where the main POTHOLES area begins. These lakes contain good numbers of bass, catfish, and perch; and because many of the lakes are created by seepage and are unconnected, trout can be successfully managed in them. Morgan and Halfmoon lakes lie a few miles northwest of Othello, and it is seldom too cold for comfort on November 1, the opening day for the trout fishing season. All kinds of waterfowl fly from lake to lake, and it's really quite an outdoors experience. Bass are all over the area. Some big rod-benders cruise the shorelines, often seeming to wait for an appealing plug. The famous POTHOLES RESERVOIR has resorts and boat rentals near O'SULLIVAN DAM and at MOSES LAKE where Rt. 90 crosses over. The best fishing for bass is in the upper reaches of the Potholes, while both trout and bass can be caught near the junction of the Potholes Reservoir and Moses Lake. This is superb fishing here, and there is more of the same west along the WINCHESTER WASTEWAY. There are boat launches on either side of Rte. 90. In early spring, terrific trout and bass fishing is found in the Quincy Lake Wildlife Refuge above the town of GEORGE. Quincy and Burke are trout lakes; and Coffin and Evergreen are bass lakes: All four have launching areas. Farther north, east of EPHRATA and SOAP LAKE on Rte. 28, the remote, picturesque BILLY CLAPP LAKE has excellent fishing for Kokanee, trout, walleye, and bass, particularly in early spring. There's a campground and good bank access on the north side and a resort to the south — near the dam. And of course, you can head north to GRAND COULEE where you can rent boats for bass and trout fishing on Banks Lake. The north half of Banks — near STEAMBOAT ROCK and in Osborn Bay — usually provides the hottest spots, though good bank fishing can be found all along Rte. 155 on the east side of Banks. This lake offers different kinds of fishing: plugging for bass, trolling for Kokanee and trout, and even cod and walleye sometimes hit when nothing else will.

THE YAKIMA RIVER

Down south on the YAKIMA RIVER, bass, steelhead, and catfish are popular. At the mouth of the Yakima at RICHLAND, bank fishing for catfish usually pays off. Upriver, bass and steelhead are caught throughout the year with the peak steelhead months in February and March, when they scale between five and twelve pounds. Good bank access points can be found on the road north from BENTON CITY. Between MABTON and GRANGER the bass fishing turns excellent, and midway between the two towns, where SATUS CREEK hits the Yakima, the local anglers often anchor boats, using salmon eggs and spin-glo artificial lures to catch steelhead in the winter. The best bass fishing in the state is on the Yakima Indian Reservation, but it is not open to the public. However, about eight miles south of Yakima below the Sunnyside Dam there are several good spots on the banks where the steelheading is simply astonishing at times.

Upstream of YAKIMA and above ROZA DAM the rainbow hit on flies, nightcrawlers, and spinners. The anglers here like to use shallow bottom boats, and again the fishing sparkles in October and November. Through the winter white fish show up, and they rival the trout. Rte. 97 bends and jogs with the Yakima River for thirty-three miles up to ELLENSBURG, and there are a number of fine Fish and Game Department access points. A good boat launch is at the town of THRALL just south of Ellensburg.

A number of really fine streams feed the Yakima River from the northwest — the BUMPING, AMERICAN, TIETON, and the NACHES. (At this point, turn to the southwestern map.) Rainbow are most common, and they ordinarily hit worms. This is a good area to take your family, with campgrounds located up Rte. 12 and Rte. 410 in the Snoqualmie National Forest. Off Rte. 12 east of RIMROCK an access road winds down along the south shore of Rimrock Lake where campgrounds and a boat launch make it an ideal spot for stopping over. Kokanee salmon stretch out to fourteen inches in length and are good and scrappy on a light line. Bait a very small hook with maggots, periwinkles, or bits of red worms. Clear Lake is a beautiful walk west of Rimrock and it holds large rainbows and brook trout. On west up Rte. 12 you will find LEECH LAKE, which is fly fishing only for trout. Or if you have chosen Rte. 410, take the turnoff south that parallels BUMPING RIVER, which is heavily stocked with trout, or stop at any inviting spot along the easily reached AMERICAN RIVER. At the end of the road many fishermen jump off for hikes into Cedar, Swamp, Twin Sisters, and Cougar Lakes. These are high-mountain lakes that it takes a good backpacker to reach, but during July and August they yield nice trout.

There is the chance for some trophy fishing up northwest of ELLENSBURG. At CLE ELUM off Rte. 90 you might hook lake trout up to twenty pounds or load up a stringer with

Kokanee. The CLE ELUM and the KACHESS LAKES both have fine resorts, but the only boat launching ramps are on KEECHELUS where you are allowed a bonus limit of twenty Kokanee.

THE EASTERN SLICE

In the southeast corner of the state, the Snake River roars through Hell's Canyon moving toward Clarkston where it turns a bit more docile. It's a fine steelhead and salmon river and offers the best fishing in these parts. Its tributary, the Grande Ronde River, is nearly as exciting. But farther north toward Spokane, the old story, "You should have been here last week — well, last month," is a common refrain during the hot summer months. A few pieces of water hold up relatively well. Some of the deeper, colder lakes in the north — Eloika, Deep, and Williams — are better bets. To the south the cool-water Tucannon River and Asotin Creek offer catchable, stocked trout.

There are numerous lakes around SPOKANE, but these so-called "metropolitan lakes" receive heavy fishing pressure. May 15 could be called the cut-off date after which limits are seldom caught, and then only if a fisherman has superior patience. Driving south on Rte. 90, you should stop at SPRAGUE to check out up-to-date reports on Amber, WILLIAMS, Badger, and Chapman Lakes. They are south of Spokane in the Turnbull National Wildlife Refuge. Comfortable stopovers, these lakes offer full accommodations. Nearer to Spokane, more resorts and trout fishing can be found at MEDICAL LAKE, Clear Lake, SILVER LAKE, and North Silver Lake.

NORTH OF SPOKANE

North of Spokane, the fishing improves with LONG LAKE on Rte. 291 and NEWMAN LAKE above Rte. 290. Newman offers good bass fishing. Probably your best chance during the summer, however, would be to drive north on Rte. 2 and rent a boat at ELOIKA LAKE where trout are plentiful. If that doesn't work, drive north on Rte. 311 to USK, cross the PEND OREILLE, go north five miles, then northeast another five miles and discover Brown's Lake and Halfmoon Lake. These are trout lakes and Brown's holds the larger fish, though it is reserved for flies only; it also has a nice campground. Driving south toward NEWPORT on Rte. 31, two more trout lakes, BEAD and Marshall, are good in spring and fall. Even better, DIAMOND LAKE has boat rentals, lodging, and some choice cutthroats. April and October are the peak months here.

Over on Rte. 395 above CLAYTON, you'll find four trout lakes. All have resorts — LOON LAKE, DEER LAKE, and WAITTS LAKE — except for small but mighty Jumpoff Joe Lake. Rte. 395 takes you to COLVILLE where you can turn right on Rte. 294 and reach several more well stocked trout lakes. The first is a lake defying its own name for visiting fishermen, Starvation Lake. North from PARK RAPIDS lies scenic, little Black Lake, which is stocked with colorful brook trout. Out of MIDDLEPORT take your pick from Thomas, Gillette,

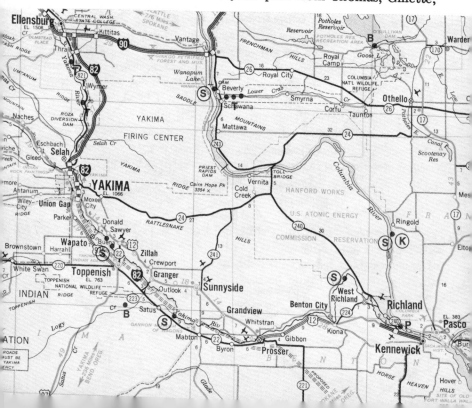

Sherry, LEO, Frater, and Niles lakes. DEEP LAKE, just south of NORTHPORT and near the Canadian border, holds excellent cutthroat and brook trout; and the fishing is fast through most of the summer. It takes some driving on secondary roads from either Ione or Northport to find the resort and public access points at the lake. North of Northport on Rte. 25, Little Sheep Creek trails along the highway and is a fun stream for wading. It holds brook trout as does Big Sheep Creek, which is usually fished by boat though it is treacherous. Crossing over ROOSEVELT LAKE and turning north on Rte. 395 to BARSTOW, cross the KETTLE RIVER and head north to PIERRE LAKE. It is a fine lake for large cutthroats, and it's attractive because of the resort and campground in a sparkling setting. Six miles south on Rte. 395, take the toll ferry at Gifford across Roosevelt Lake. Right out in the middle of nowhere you'll find TWIN LAKES, which is superb trout fishing. At INCHELIUM you can obtain special Indian permits to fish or launch a boat on their waters. A resort is there too.

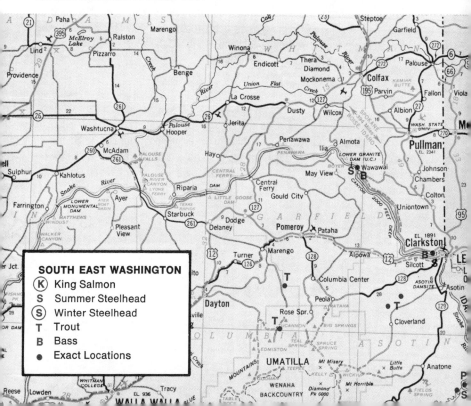

THE FAR SOUTHEAST

South and northwest of CLARKSTON — down in the southeastern corner — the SNAKE RIVER offers you lunker smallmouth bass. They are wary, but crawdads and spinners will sometimes fool them. There are many access points to the Snake, and it has most kinds of fish. You can put a boat in at WAWAWAI, or you can go to Rogersburg and fish the juncture of the Snake and Grande Ronde rivers, particularly during the fall steelhead run. This is also a fine place to arrange for jet-boat trips up through Hell's Canyon. We won't go on about the canyon other than to say you won't be worrying too much about the fishing on that trip.

Driving south on Rte. 129 out of CLARKSTON, you will find one of the best spots for fall steelheading — it takes the summer run awhile to get this far inland — where the road crosses the GRANDE RONDE. The only other reasonably good fishing around here would be for catchable trout in the Tucannon River west of COLUMBIA CENTER and in the Asotin Creek west of ASOTIN. These are nice, free-flowing waters, and if nothing else they will at least cool your feet after a day behind the wheel.

This is a big country with a lot of water and a lot of fish. Some of the fishing holes are incredibly beautiful places. Some of the fish possess unusual amounts of heart and fight. Some of your expeditions will bring all of these exhilarating factors together simultaneously, and suddenly all of your effort will have been worthwhile.